S0-ALH-000

"HM? I FIND YOU QUITE SATISFACTORY, THOUGH. I'D BE MORE THAN HAPPY TO MARRY YOU. DIDN'T YOU NOTICE? I LIKE YOU A LOT, TOUYA..."

LEEN JUMPED UP AND PEERED RIGHT INTO MY EYES. JUST AS I WAS ABOUT TO COMMENT ON HER CLOSENESS, I FELT A LITTLE KISS.

In Another World With My Smartphone 8

"WILL TOUYA AND FRIENDS BE ABLE TO OVERCOME THIS LATEST CHALLENGE....!?"

# BABYLON WORLD!"

"HYAAHH! HEY, YOU LITTLE...! LET ME GO!"

"KYAAAHHHHH!"

I TURNED TO THE SCREAMS AGAIN AND NOTICED THAT BOTH ELZE AND LU HAD JOINED YAE AND HILDE IN BEING SUSPENDED FROM TENTACLES.

# In Another World With My Smartphone

Patora Fuyuhara
illustration·Eiji Usatsuka

IN ANOTHER WORLD WITH MY SMARTPHONE: VOLUME 8
by Patora Fuyuhara

Translated by Andrew Hodgson
Edited by DxS

This book is a work of fiction. Names, characters, places, and incidents are the product of the author's imagination or are used fictitiously. Any resemblance to actual events, locales, or persons, living or dead, is coincidental.

Original Japanese edition published in 2016 by Hobby Japan
This English edition is published by arrangement with Hobby Japan, Tokyo

English translation © 2018 J-Novel Club LLC

Find more books like this one at www.j-novel.club!

President and Publisher: Samuel Pinansky
Managing Editor: Aimee Zink

ISBN: 978-1-7183-5007-6
Printed in Korea
First Printing: February 2020
10 9 8 7 6 5 4 3 2 1

# Contents

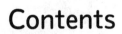

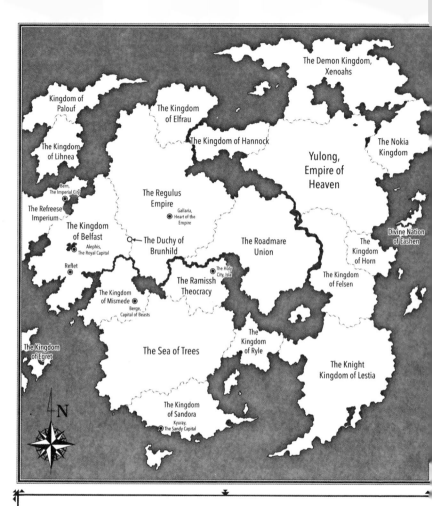

# The Story So Far!

Mochizuki Touya, wielding a smartphone customized by God himself, has made a name for himself in the new world. He is now grand duke of Brunhild, a nation formed of territory from both the Kingdom of Belfast and the Regulus Empire. Having rightfully inherited the ancient legacy of Babylon, Touya now commands a fleet of enormous humanoid mechs known as Frame Gears. Using these Frame Gears, he attempts to make contact with all the countries of the world in order to defend against the Phrase, monstrous invaders from another world. Amidst all of this political turmoil, Touya must yet brace for the oncoming winter. Unbeknownst to our stalwart young grand duke, however, is the fact that the season won't be the only thing that changes...

Ever since Lestia joined the Western Alliance, the official name was changed to the East-West Alliance to reflect its new status.

And as of today, the Knight King Reinhard would be taking his seat at the council.

"I am honored to be here among you, though I hope my inexperience in these matters will not be too much of a burden."

"You don't need to worry about that. The whole point of this gathering is for us all to share our opinions as equals and help each other out, so just feel free to say whatever's on your mind." The Pope met the King of Knights' courteous introduction with a gentle smile. This whole thing had turned into a sort of club before I realized it, but we *were* technically using it to discuss important matters, so I was just kind of rolling with it at this point.

"I've only recently succeeded the throne myself, you see. I hope we can get along."

"As do I, Your Majesty."

The newly appointed Kings of Lihnea and Lestia shared a firm handshake. There was surely plenty for them to learn from each other. I mean, I was technically royalty myself now, but I was pretty sure I'd make a terrible role model, so I figured it was in everyone's best interests for them not to follow *my* examples too much.

"Seeing Lestia join us as allies is startling enough already, but I hear you've even recently won over the tribes of the Sea of Trees.

You never fail to take me by surprise, Touya." The Beast King of Mismede decided to join in on the young Kings' conversation. *Man, word on that really travelled fast, huh? Though I guess I shouldn't be too surprised given the number of beastmen in Mismede. From what I've heard they've been keeping in touch with the tribes inhabiting the Sea of Trees for a while anyway, so he probably just heard it straight from the horse's mouth, so to speak.*

"I dunno if I'd say I 'won them over' or anything like that. I just kind of ended up helping them out and then they thanked me for it. I don't really plan on sticking my nose into their business." I didn't really see any reason to hide it, so I followed this up by explaining what exactly had transpired.

I told them everything, from the state of the refugees who had drifted in from Yulong, to a recent incident in which I loaned out a Frame Gear to help clear up the passage that'd gotten blocked off due to a landslide. Once that was all out of the way, everyone took Reinhard to the baseball stadium to go watch today's main event: an exhibition match to welcome our newest member, the team matchup of the day being Refreese vs. Regulus.

As the guardsmen and soldiers all headed towards the arena, I suddenly remembered something I should probably mention to the Pope. I called out to her in a hushed voice so as not to attract too much attention from our surroundings.

"Your Holiness, I just felt I should mention this, but uh… Well, actually, there are two Gods here today, in human form, of course, but still… Would you like me to introduce you to them?"

"Eh, really!?" Unable to hide her surprise, she nodded vigorously at my proposal. I took her along to visit my older sisters, Karen and Moroha, who were drinking tea at a nearby table. I introduced one very nervous Pope to the two Gods, and in turn, the two Gods to one very nervous Pope.

"These girls are my older sisters... Or, well, that's the story we're rolling with. They're actually the God of Love and the God of Swords, respectively."

"Touya, it's kinda creepy when you actually treat us like Gods for once, y'know?"

"Yeah, I really don't know how to respond when you put me on the spot like this. Let's just take it chill, alright? That goes for you too, little lady. Just seeing you get all worked up like that is hard to watch." My sisters caught the Pope just as she was about to prostrate herself on the floor before them, and led her into a seat at the table instead. Following the introductions, the Pope began asking all sorts of questions about the Gods and the Divine Realm — tripping over her words every now and then, but still, seeing my sisters answering so lightheartedly while munching on sweets must've helped her calm down a little, because they at least seemed to be having a somewhat lively conversation amongst themselves. I couldn't help but wonder if women were just quicker to adapt to groups of the same sex like this.

I briefly wondered if this fell under the category of interfering with matters of the human realm, but I figured it was probably fine since they weren't exactly using their divine powers just to have some light conversation.

*I mean, I suppose this could technically be construed as her receiving some kind of Divine Revelations... But I've never heard of any such silly Revelations as 'The God of Commerce is way too petty' or 'The God of Liquor needs to dial it back with the heavy drinking' before in my life. It's probably fine to just leave them to their conversation while I go watch the game.*

Having judged it safe to leave the Pope with my sisters, I made my way to the stadium.

The whole place was already getting heated up for the first real match in a month.

I could spot people among the audience from not just our country, but people who seemed like they'd come all the way from Refreese and Regulus to see the match as well. People selling popcorn and beer were running around turning a huge profit, as the audience swung between cheers of joy and cries of disappointment all in unison. I could never have predicted just how well this would go down with the people of this world when I first came up with the idea.

In the VIP seating area, Reinhard was already completely glued to the game. He reminded me of when Cloud saw his first match, too. Speaking of Cloud, Reinhard could occasionally be spotted asking him questions about the game as the two shared their opinions on the match unfolding like some kind of running commentary.

Maybe because they had both only succeeded their respective thrones relatively recently, but the two of them seemed to be getting along already. It'd be nice if they became good friends like the King of Belfast and the Emperor of Refreese.

*Speaking of Refreese, I can already picture that princess getting a nosebleed and writing all sorts of indecent books if she were to catch even a glimpse of this scene. I mean, hell, they're both the spitting image of storybook Prince Charmings (King Charmings in this case, the point stands)... Tch. Even with plenty of girls ready to become my wives, a man is still allowed to be jealous of handsome fellas like that. What? Don't you judge me.*

A loud, clear sound followed by a tremendous cheer snapped me back to my senses. The Regulus team's batter had just hit a home run. Players who could hit a home run at the critical moment like that never failed to get the crowd going.

Reinhard even leaped out of his seat with excitement. On the other hand, the King of Belfast, being a good friend of the Emperor of Refreese, hung his head in dismay at the sight, almost as if the very ball soaring into the air had soared straight into his gut instead.

All friendly sports rivalry aside, I was glad to see everyone getting along with each other. I decided to make a full kit of baseball equipment to give to Reinhard once the match was over.

The next day, I woke up to a wave of biting cold and a real winter wonderland spreading outside of my window before my eyes.

Yup, that's right. Snow. A whole lot of it, at that. Not enough to have blocked the doors shut, but it still had to be at least ten centimeters high.

The training grounds for the soldiers were virtually unusable in this condition, though, so the knights were shoveling the snow out of both the training grounds and barracks areas. I suggested just melting it all away with some fire magic, but I got told to think a little about how turning snow into water was going to help the problem at all. In retrospect that definitely wouldn't have been my brightest moment.

I decided to go check on the state of the townsfolk as well, and just like the knights, the adults were busy shoveling the snow outside the front of their houses. Meanwhile, the children were having fun with snowball fights.

I got invited to play with them, and having no reason to refuse, I decided to teach them about other fun things you could do to play in the snow. First, I took an empty wooden box and some planks of wood and built a simple little sled. Next, I took all of the shoveled snow and made a little hill out of it for the kids to slide down. Once they learned about it, they were hooked on this new game straight away.

Leaving the kids to have fun with their new toy, I went out to check on the main roads. Just as I thought, the roads were snowed in to the point I could barely tell it was supposed to be a road. Guess this meant we wouldn't be seeing any merchants passing through for a while. Well, assuming it doesn't snow anymore then the roads would probably be plenty usable again after the snow melts over the next two or three days.

It wasn't every day we got snow like this, so I decided to head on over to the baseball stadium to see if there was anything fun I could make out of this.

*3 simple steps to constructing your own makeshift ice-skating rink: First, level out the mounds of the baseball field buried underneath the snow. Next, lightly melt a thin layer of the snow until you get an even coating of water across the field. And finally, re-freeze the melted snow while keeping the surface as flat as possible. And just like that, you're done!*

"Yup, looking pretty good. Let's see if it's solid enough to st-AAAAND WAH!" I had barely taken a step onto the ice rink before completely losing my footing and being sent tumbling onto my back. *Is this some kind of karmic payback for all those people I've tormented with my [Slip] spell until now!? That* really *hurt!*

"…What the blazes are you up to *this* time?" inquired Logan, who — judging by the shovels he and the knights behind him were carrying — had probably come to dig out the baseball stadium's field.

And what's worse, it looked like they saw everything... I probably wasn't gonna live this one down for a while, but oh well.

"Oh, y'know, just thought I'd make a simple ice skating rink."

"Eyes Gating Ring? Some kind of new magic?"

"Eh? You seriously don't have them over here? Y'know, where you slide about on top of the ice in boots with little blades attached to the bottom."

"Oh, you mean the Gliding Arts. Come to think of it, they use that technique a lot in the northern kingdom of Elfrau. I hear that the waterways tend to freeze over in the winter up there, so they make the best of that by sliding around over the surface of them to get around faster." In other words, this world had something similar, but they had only ever seen it as an alternative form of transport. It made sense since that was definitely a fast way of getting around, but they didn't seem to have considered that it could be pretty fun to just enjoy the sensation of sliding around on the ice. Now I *had* to introduce this to them.

I started off by whipping up a simple pair of skating boots by fastening some makeshift blades to the bottom of my shoes, and then stepping onto the rink to demonstrate. Unlike before, I glided somewhat more gracefully over the icy surface this time.

I heard several voices of amazement at my skills, but all I was really doing was skating in a straight line... But it did make me want to show off a little, so I did a couple rounds of the outer circumference of the arena while doing simple little spins and stunts here and there. *Don't underestimate a kid raised in the north, wahaha! Well, I say that, but my hometown was on the side of Japan nearer to the Pacific Ocean, so I don't have the crazy resistance to the cold that you find in people further up north...*

I made a full set of blades for Logan and the others and handed them over. They were a sort of clip-on type that you attached to the bottom of your own shoes as opposed to the kind of skating boots that come with the blades permanently affixed. As the guys timidly stepped out onto the ice rink, they began tumbling all over the place like a scene straight out of an old cartoon. *Ha ha ha! Bet you won't be laughing at my little slip-up from earlier anymore, will you!?*

But before I could fully enjoy the silly sight, everyone gradually grew more and more accustomed to it with just a little bit of practice.

The people of this world never failed to surprise me with how quickly they grew accustomed to my new tricks and toys. Then again, they were all pretty athletic to begin with, so I really should've seen this coming. Before I knew it, even the townsfolk had begun to show up to watch our Knight Order gracefully gliding around my ice skating rink. I figured it'd be more fun to just let everyone participate at will, so I whipped up a large batch of attachable skating blades and just left them out for people to make free use of since it would've been a pain handing them all out one-by-one.

"Urgh... What have I done?" I groaned grumpily while sitting on one of the stadium benches. After only a short time had passed, my ice skating rink had slowly but surely begun filling up with young couples and married couples. My fun playground had turned into a hot-spot for romantic couples right under my nose.

Singles despaired at the sight and gradually began leaving one after another, whose skating blades were then taken up by new couples who had arrived to join the others above the ice. It was a vicious, lonely cycle.

Amongst this, though, the heroes of the loner singles' ranks saw this as a chance to invite girls out onto the rink and teach them how to skate.

The whole place was totally just one big date spot by now. Well, the younger kids seemed to be having plenty of innocent, childish fun with it, so it wasn't *all* just a couples' event.

Upon closer inspection, I noticed a disproportionate number of girls who didn't seem to be able to skate, inevitably invited out onto the rink by guys who had already completely mastered the basics offering to teach them. Just like that, they'd be off hand-in-hand to go have a good time with each other… In other words, the guys saw it as the perfect chance to go around hitting on girls.

When I thought about it, though, it did sort of make sense. Under the guise of a noble act of kindness in teaching girls how to skate, the guys had the perfect excuse to join hands with cute girls without drawing any unwanted attention for it. It was pretty crafty when I thought of it like that.

Among the girls seemed to be those who had figured this out, too, and were quite clearly faking being unable to skate so that they could attract men like the others. Well, as long as both parties were okay with it, I figured this was one of those times where the correct course of action was to just avoid bringing it up since it'd just ruin everyone's fun.

"I had a feeling I'd find you at the heart of all this commotion, Touya."

"I don't know how I feel about being your number one suspect whenever crowds start to gather for any reason, but well, yeah, can't deny that this one was my handiwork." When Yumina showed up out of nowhere to tease me yet again, I decided it was wisest to just roll with it at this point. *I mean, I don't think I'm the source of all of the commotion in this world*, I thought to myself, *but she's right on the mark this time.*

Now that I had a partner myself, I saw no real reason to skip out on the experience of an ice skating date myself. I gave Yumina a pair of skating blades and we headed right out onto the rink.

"Care to join me for a skate, My Princess?"

"...Do you think I'll be able to do it? It looks rather difficult..." Yumina inquired nervously. I couldn't really blame her, since this was her first time and all. For the time being, I led her out onto the rink by the hand and taught her the tricks behind it one small step at a time.

She seemed unsure how to keep her balance at first, but she gradually grew used to the new sensation and was gliding around beautifully before I knew it. I was ready to pin it on the naturally athletic nature of the people in this world, but thinking about it more critically, I started to wonder if maybe the reason this kept surprising me was because my old world had been such a convenient place that the people had just become more and more complacent over the years.

At this time, I had no way of knowing that ice skating dates would become one of the standard winter attractions of my very own Duchy of Brunhild.

"You found more of the Babylon ruins? Where?"

"I did. They are located in the middle of the Demon Kingdom Xenoahs, in a mountainous area." Kougyoku reported this information to me, and I fell into deep thought.

The Demon Kingdom of Xenoahs… It was a secluded nation inhabited by Demonkin.

Under the Demon King's rule, they were a country that strongly avoided interacting with the outside world. Despite being a treacherous area with plenty of natural defenses due to its unique geography, it was said that all sorts of races lived there in peace. Not just Demonkin, but many subspecies of monsters and magical beasts are said to roam the area in great numbers. There were all sorts of dangerous rumors about the place.

I was hesitant to charge blindly into unknown territory, so I called out one of the Demonkin from my Knight Order to see if he could give me any useful information about the place.

"Xenoahs, you say?" The boy I called out was a young Vampire with red eyes, fair white skin, and pointed ears. His name was Lushade.

Despite being a Vampire, he was a bit of an eccentric who couldn't really stand the sight of blood. According to him, blood was more like a luxury food for Vampires rather than being essential for their survival.

He was a guy who single-handedly destroyed the image of Vampires I'd always held inside my head. For one thing, the sun didn't bother him at all. He thoroughly enjoyed meals prepared with garlic as some of his favorite dishes. He could handle crosses or crucifixes just fine, and silver weapons were about as effective on him as they would be on pretty much anyone else. He couldn't transform into a bat, and to top it all off, he couldn't even stand the sight of blood.

Apart from Lushade's own eccentric distaste for blood, it seemed that all the Vampires in this world were pretty much the same as him. Heck, people who'd had their blood sucked by vampires wouldn't even turn into vampires themselves in this world.

Apparently they were still blessed with many powerful abilities, such as incredible night-vision, superhuman strength, and tremendous self-recovery abilities to name a few... But looking at this young man, I found that pretty hard to picture in my head.

At any rate, I'd heard that Vampires tended to hold considerably high social status within Xenoahs, which was why I called Lushade out hoping I might be able to glean some useful information from him.

To this day, it remained a mystery to me why someone of such a high social standing would come all the way out here just to join my Knight Order. When we interviewed him for the position, I seemed to recall him saying something about wanting to gain his own independence in his life.

"So, like, are there no humans in Xenoahs at all?"

"No, there are a few. Even some Demi-Humans live there. Just because Xenoahs keeps itself from getting involved in other countries' affairs doesn't mean it totally isolates itself from the outside world altogether. It's just that it's an incredibly difficult place for just about *any* race to live in."

"Whaddya mean?"

"Well, first and not least of all the climate is somewhat extreme there. The temperature at midday gets scorching hot, meanwhile the nights can reach sub-zero temperatures easily. Not to mention the fact that magic beasts inhabit the land in droves. Just stepping outside of town means you're almost guaranteed to be attacked by whole packs of them. Plus there's the problem of the food supply. There isn't exactly much that most humans would willingly eat unless they had no other choice. I mean, would *you* willingly eat Slime Jelly or Orc meat?" *Orc meat? By Orcs, he means those orcs, right? The ones with pig heads and humanoid bodies? Can you actually eat those things!? I mean come on! You should at least be eating regular pork in that case! As for Slime Jelly... Yeah, no thanks. That just sounds outright disgusting. Like he said, I can see why their local cuisine would be pretty tough for ordinary humans to get used to...*

"...Do Orcs not count as Demonkin?"

"Of course not. They can't even communicate with words, remember? Demons refers to races with high enough intelligence to at least hold a coherent conversation. Everything else gets classified as either magic beasts or monsters." His explanation made sense.

I asked Lushade if there were any slightly more... *appetizing* foods to choose from, at which point he brought up Mini-Wyrm Soup and Grilled Giant Bats and such. I could feel my stomach turning just hearing about it. There's no way in hell I could bring myself to eat that stuff, not even if you paid me a hundred platinum as a dare. Heck, for all I knew they might be delicious, but the appearance alone would be guaranteed to kill my appetite altogether.

"That said, it actually took me a little while to get accustomed to the cuisine over here, too. It's nice now that I'm used to it, but sometimes I do find myself longing for my home country's cooking again," said Lushade as he made a forced smile. *Guess it's true what they say about longing for the taste of your hometown,* I thought to myself.

Pushing this disturbing talk of horrific foodstuffs out of my mind, I recalled my main objective. If there were humans living in the country already, then I supposed I might not stand out as much as I originally thought if I were to take a trip there. I figured I could maybe sneak my way into the country easily enough in order to go investigate those Ruins of Babylon.

If I got caught I could just come up with some excuse like being a penniless wandering noble. I wasn't planning on stirring up any trouble, and it's not like my outward appearance made me look like anyone of particular importance or anything.

With that, I decided to take a quick expedition to scout the place out. Unfortunately Lushade had never been directly to the ruins himself, so I'd have to just jump to Yulong and use my [Fly] spell to cover the rest of the distance.

Since I was travelling by flight this time, I had the rest of the party wait back at the castle. Just in case anything happened and I had to contact anyone for support I decided to take Kohaku or one of the others with me, but since I could only take one of them it came very close to breaking out into a fight between them. Breaking up their little spat was a pain in the ass.

Yumina drew up a lottery to help make the decision as fair as possible, which ended up with Kohaku being the one to accompany me this time. With that decided, I opened up a [Gate] to Yulong. The very same place we'd fought the Phrase once before.

*Same old wasteland as usual,* I thought to myself. With nothing to do here, we set out for our original goal without hesitation. After casting [Levitation] on Kohaku, I fired up my [Fly] spell and we headed straight for Xenoahs.

Just for added safety, so we didn't get caught and/or restrained as suspicious individuals, I made sure to cast [**Invisible**] on us both. Could never be too careful in unknown territory.

The moment we entered Xenoahs airspace, something came flying straight in our direction. For a moment I feared we had been spotted already, but on closer inspection that didn't seem to be the case. Just to avoid any unnecessary risks, I slowed down our flying speed and decided to observe from a distance for a while. It was then that I noticed that what had been heading our way was two Demonkin. The upper halves of their bodies were those of women, while their arms and legs were those of birds.

"Those are Harpies. The talons on their feet have enough force to rip bears apart, but they're unlikely to attack us unless we were to provoke them first." Just like Kohaku said, the Harpies flew right past us without so much as a glance in our direction. Come to think about it, they wouldn't even have been able to track us down by spell due to the magic fields we had up to help conceal our presence completely.

From what I could tell, Harpies must've been a species of Demon. They certainly didn't look like magical beasts to me, at least. I was still a little unclear on what separated Demons from magical beasts, but according to Lushade, anything humanoid that you could hold a coherent conversation with would be a Demon, whereas creatures like the Dullahan where communication with them was totally impossible were monsters. Meanwhile, non-humanoid creatures that you could still communicate with such as Unicorns still fell under the category of magical beasts. I still didn't fully understand all the distinctions between them, but I felt like I had a least a basic grasp of the logic behind it by now.

"Let's try to err on the side of caution, just in case. There's no telling what sorts of strange magic beasts we might run into all the way out here, and I'm willing to bet there's a lot of them that we've never had to deal with before." Once the Harpies were out of view, we continued our flight toward our destination. Gazing upon the scenery below us revealed nothing but wastelands, treacherous mountains, and thick wooded areas for as far as the eye could see. I was beginning to understand why living in such a place would be such a challenge for the average person.

There were routes resembling paths dotted around here and there, but even those looked treacherous enough as though they were just there due to being well-tread over the years, as opposed to being deliberately made to make passage between two specific areas any easier or safer.

"This place looks plenty unforgiving enough for the uninitiated already. I mean, I expect the capital won't look anything like these backwoods roads, but I can see where these lands get their intimidating reputation from."

"The magical particles are thick in the air around these parts, which may be what's attracting the magic beasts in such great numbers. It's definitely the kind of place where humans would struggle even to survive a few days, from what I can see. Demon races with their unnatural resistance and physical resilience would be another story, but other races would likely not fare so well in these conditions…" In a way, that description made it sound to me like exactly the kind of ideal environment to establish a country of Demonkin in.

*Still, isn't it a bit too hot here? I could've sworn it was the middle of winter when we left Brunhild… I mean, the sun's blasting on at full power and might even blind me if I'm not careful. Does it get some kind of status power-up in the skies of this area or something? Could it be due to the density of magical particles in the air around here, or does it maybe have something to do with the Earth Spirits in this part of the world?*

*It's times like this I'm glad my jacket has resistance to the natural elements,* I thought to myself, secretly paying thanks to my long-time partner.

Snapping myself out of my sightseeing tour, I noticed something else flying in our direction. *More Harpies,* I wondered? Looking closer, they were large blue birds resembling condors. Those must've been some of Kougyoku's followers.

Upon dispelling my [**Invisible**] spell, the birds seemed to recognize us and changed direction to fly eastward as if to guide us to where we were going.

Eventually we reached a mountainous area, and the birds took us to a small valley.

"What's this…?" Nestled in a nook between mountains, there was a large structure that resembled the Arc de Triomphe.

I descended and checked out the structure's composition. It was definitely made out of the same stuff as the others. It seemed we were right to assume.

It was about three meters tall, and when I passed under it I found myself in a small room with letters engraved on the wall. To my left hand side there were five different objects stacked up in a row.

The middle of the room had a small stone pillar that went up to my waist. There was a fire spellstone sitting atop it. It kind of resembled a hokora, a small Shinto shrine for offerings. It was made out of the same stuff as the rest of the structure, though.

"Hm… This is definitely new. What's this all about…?" I channeled magic into the stone, but that didn't work. I heard a loud buzzer sound, signifying I'd done something wrong. It felt just like the kind of sound you'd hear on a quiz show if someone made a wrong answer. I figured this was the ruin's way of telling me I was doing it wrong. "Hm... Maybe those symbols are a clue. Oh... I should read the letters... [**Reading**]: **Ancient Spirit Script!**" Just like that, the letters became legible.

"Let's see... 'Line up the shapes to the right in the correct order, top to bottom. You do not need to physically move them. Simply imagining it as you channel your magic into the firestone is enough.' What..." *What's going on...? A quiz? Are the shapes those weird things stacked up on the wall to the left?*

There was a square, a semi-circle, a star, a full circle, and a triangle. All had dots on them, too. Five for the square, three for the semi-circle, one for the star, four for the circle, and two for the triangle.

"If these dots are the key to it... Could it really be that simple?" I pictured the shapes in my mind in the following order. Star, triangle, semi-circle, circle, square. Then I poured my magical power into the stone. *Bzzt.* I was wrong. Well, that would've been too easy.

"...Maybe it's by number of straight sides?" The circle had no straight edges, the semi-circle had one, triangle had three, square had four... and star had five. There wasn't a shape with two, though. It was kind of annoying. *Man, I'm not really getting this at all...* Regardless, I tried the order of circle, semi-circle, triangle, square, star.

*Bzzt.* Wrong again!

"Damn it... Is it really the dots, then?"

"Perhaps the shapes represent different meanings."

"Uh… Meanings? The circle… Maybe that's the sun…? Then the semi-circle is the moon… Then the star is… a star… Is it some kind of astrological thing? What about the triangle and square?!" *Maybe if I'm arranging them top to bottom… It's their distance from the planet? So the furthest is the stars, then the sun… Then the moon… If the triangle is a house…? And the square is the planet itself!* I tried lining them up like that.

*Bzzt.*

"Ugh… Come on… The dots have to be the hints, but what does it mean?!"

After that, I spent some time glaring at the shapes. It became a tedious process of trial and error. But mostly error. A long while passed, until…

*Ding ding ding!!*

"WHAT?! GIMME A GODDAMN BREAK!"

"M-My liege… I understand your frustration, but please calm yourself." A loud rumbling came as the wall of shapes moved to the side, opening for me. Frankly I wished I could've kicked it down. Kohaku's imploring stopped me, though.

"That was such a stupid question! What the hell kind of answer was that supposed to be?!"

"I-I agree, but still…" Kohaku sighed in resignation. The answer to the puzzle infuriated me. It was simple enough… "There are no shapes to the right." That was it. I felt like an idiot. But it was true. The shapes were to my left, and the question asked me to sort shapes to my right… It was just a stupid riddle! I calmed myself down and progressed inwards to the next room. I found myself facing a familiar sight. A wall with lettering carved into it, and a pillar with a blue spellstone in the middle of the room. *NOT AGAIN!*

"There are eight coins and a single scale. One of the coins is counterfeit. The counterfeit coin weighs a little bit less than a legitimate coin, thus it is easy to discover by weighing. The question, however, is what is the least number of attempts needed to determine the false coin? An incorrect answer will return you to the entrance." *This one's a little trickier... Gonna need to think about this.*

*It shouldn't take much brainpower though! That's right, the answer is... Wait... Hold on, uh...*

I channeled my magical power into the blue spellstone as I pictured the answer in my mind.

*Ding ding ding, we have a winner!*

*Just as I expected... It was trying to trick me.* I narrowed my eyes slightly as the next wall opened up.

"My lord, what was the answer?"

Kohaku looked up at me, curious. *Hm? You didn't get it?*

"Well, think about it. How many tries should it take?"

"Well, the first try should be spent weighing four coins on each side. Then you should spend the second try dividing the lighter four into piles of two, and weighing them. Third and final, you weigh the final two coins from the lighter side again. It will take three attempts total."

"I see... That's technically true, yes. But you could take six coins and measure them in two piles of three. If they were balanced, it would mean one of the two left over was the counterfeit. Then you'd only need a second try to confirm the answer. If they weren't balanced, then it'd just be a matter of placing one coin from the lighter pile on either side. If those were balanced, then the remaining one would be the fake. If they were imbalanced, the fake would be

29

the lighter one. Either way, it would take two measurements. That's the generally accepted answer, I think." *Emphasis on generally...*

"Then you mean to imply it could be done in less than two?"

"The answer is it takes one. You can randomly take two coins from the eight, and measure their weight. If you're lucky enough you'll be able to find it in one go."

"What? Luck?"

"The question didn't specify anything like having a guarantee of success, it just asked the least number of times the scale could be used." *Just the kind of nonsense I'd expect from a Babylon ruin. It's unpleasant all the way through... It really reminds me of how the woman herself acts. I feel a little dirty, like I know how she ticks now... I'm a little uneasy about that, but... It feels like I know her well.*

*Some time later...* "Please follow the rules of the current calculation. In this system, what does X equal?" 36 = 1, 108 = 3, 2160 = 2, 10800 = X. The question seemed fairly straightforward, and I was unsure about whether or not she'd hidden some kind of devious trick within it.

But in the end, there was no trick. The answer was merely 5.

It wasn't really much of a puzzle, just a standard question. It wasn't difficult or anything, either. I couldn't afford to get them wrong and find myself back at the entrance, though. The wall opened up again, and I headed to my next problem. I wanted them to stop.

*Ding ding ding... We have a winner!*

I finally broke through the last room, one with a null spellstone, and found myself facing a familiar magic circle.

"Finally... That took way longer than it should have..." Even if it was just a stupid prank from the Doctor, it was a real pain in the ass. I grumbled quietly as I let magic flow from my body into the six stone pillars. Then, making sure Kohaku was with me in the middle of the circle, I let the Null magic spill out at my feet.

A flash of light engulfed us before gradually fading. I opened my eyes to find myself viewing the familiar sight of Babylon. The sky was calm and cloudy, and I could see trees swaying in the breeze.

I looked around, curious, and spotted a building far away. I wondered if I'd found the Storehouse, the Library, or maybe even the Research Lab.

I started walking towards the building and, gradually, I came to get a good look at it.

It was round, like a big can of tuna. But the most striking thing about it was that it was entirely made of glass. I could see everything inside. What I saw was bookshelves. Dozens of them, perhaps hundreds. The interior was so full of shelves packed with books that I could barely comprehend what I was looking at.

I'd found the Library, that much was clear.

I walked around the building, searching for a way inside. Eventually, I found a massive set of double doors.

I pushed them open, only to find another door on the inside. After I opened that and stepped through I found myself in the Library proper.

"Whoa…"

"Goodness…" Kohaku and I were taken aback. There were books everywhere. Books as far as the eye could see.

The rows upon rows of bookshelves were all at least ten meters tall. The place almost felt like a maze of literature.

Plus, I couldn't see any kind of ladder or stepping system, so I had no idea how I was supposed to even reach the highest shelves.

I walked around on the fancy red carpet, attempting to make my way to the center of the building. Naturally it wasn't so easy as just walking there in a straight line; I had to navigate the awkward bookshelves. I wondered whether or not that was intentional.

Still, looking up at the ceiling helped me get an idea of where I was headed.

After a while of exploring past book after book, we came out in a clearing amongst the shelving. There was a single desk and chair. There was a huge pile of books on top of the desk, and buried amongst them was a girl.

She seemed to be quite engrossed in one of the tomes, refusing to look up for even a moment. Her hair was cut short, colored an icy blue, and she wore glasses on her face. Overall she looked similar in dress and stature to the others I'd encountered before, so I made the assumption she was the Library's Terminal Gynoid.

"Uh…"

"I will be finished with this book in approximately thirty minutes. Until then, do not attempt discourse with me."

"Uh, right…" *She's cold. Treating me like a pest, huh? I mean… Should I just wait?*

I sat in the quiet room, the occasional sound of a turning page haunting my ears. I was bored, so I decided to pick up a book and look through it.

As I turned the page, the paper quality struck me as unusual. *Hm… What's with this? This is a seriously old book… Wait, what's with the letters?*

"I can't read this at all…" *Hm… What language is this? It doesn't look like spirit script or the ancient magical tongue… Is it the language they spoke in Partheno?* **"[Reading]: Ancient Partheno Language."** *Oh, got it. But… Oh. I can't even understand what it's talking about… Some kinda complicated report about magical beasts or something…?*

Still, I'd cast the spell now, so I could freely browse the titles of the nearby books and finally have an idea of what they actually said. That meant that every book here was in Partheno's ancient tongue.

"Mystical Fluid Manipulation For Dummies..."

"Secret Magic Herbs and Spices..."

"Sure-fire Naughty Night Tips, Beginners Manual..." *Hm...* The title had caught my eye, so I reached out to that one and gave it a look. It was, as it had first seemed, a simple how-to guide.

"The primary issue is alleviating tension. You can both indulge in one another if you're more relaxed... Provided you're of age, try drinking a little alcohol to loosen up. Not too much, though. Too much alcohol will cause a disaster, so practice intoxication in moderation. Step Two: How to touch their..." *Hmhm... Hohoho... I... I see, yes... This is good... This is... Surprisingly... Informative, yes... Oh my... Wait, you can do that? That... That goes there? Hm... This is difficult, being casual seems to require a lot of prep...*

"Enjoying your book, are you?"

"Gah!!" I jolted upwards at the sudden voice. *Woah, what?! Agh! H-Has it really been a whole half hour already?!* The girl looked at me, clearly puzzled, as she tilted her head.

"Welcome to the Babylon Library. I am the Terminal Gynoid of this institution, Irisfam. You, however, may refer to me as Fam."

"O-Oh, right... I'm Mochizuki Touya. Nice to meet you, Fam." I put the book I had taken back on its shelf, desperately hoping the girl hadn't seen what it was.

"Well, you're here... That means you've solved all of the Doctor's riddles. Thus, Airframe Number Twenty-Four, Irisfam, will have her ownership rights transferred to you. I look forward to working with you, Master." Just as I'd thought, Doctor Babylon really was responsible for those stupid questions. *Why would she even do that?*

IN ANOTHER WORLD WITH MY SMARTPHONE

*It was just annoying... Still, it's much better than all that dumb erotic stuff she made me do earlier... That was the w— hagh!!* Before I could finish that thought, Fam's lips were pressed up against mine. Our saliva mingled as she penetrated past my lips with her sticky tongue, swirling it around my own. Unlike Liora, however, she kept the union rather brief.

"Registration completed. Your genes are stored in my bank, Master. Thus, the Library is formally your property." *I should've expected this. Why didn't I prepare for this? Well, it's not like I had any choice in the matter... She'd have extracted my genetic sample one way or the other, so kissing was probably the best outcome for everyone.*

"Well then, I'd like to know. How many Babylons have been assembled?"

"Hm? Oh, uh... I have the Garden, the Workshop, the Alchemy Lab, the Hangar, the Tower, the Rampart... Now I have the Library! That makes seven."

"Oh. Come with me, then." Fam typed something into the terminal at the central desk, and the Library suddenly came alive. It began moving, probably to dock with the others over Brunhild.

"Master. I've a request. The Library requires more books, you see."

"More? Aren't there enough here already?"

"The Library is currently stocked with twenty million books." *What?! Even the National Diet Library in Japan only has around ten million... Although if you include stuff like newspapers, magazines, and stuff like that, it's probably over thirty million.*

"I have read everything in the Library. That is why it is urgent that I have some fresh material."

"Wait... You've read twenty million books?"

34

"On average it takes me two hours to read a single book. I have been doing so for the past five-thousand years." *That's absolutely insane. Do you not sleep or something?! Cesca and Flora were sleeping or in stasis or whatever, and even Noel sleeps regularly... What are you made of?!* "I do not move much at all, so I expend little in the way of energy. That being said, I have operated autonomously for five-thousand years. Once we have the Research Lab, I will require necessary maintenance." *Reading books for over five-thousand years... She's pretty hardcore. Guess she must really love literature... Still, not exactly the kind of person I expected to meet here.*

I decided to return home and report in that I'd found the Library. After all, Leen had been waiting for this for a very long time...

"I-It's time!! It's happening! It's finally happening!!" A girl dressed in gothic lolita fashion was jumping around excitedly, waving her arms in the air. Naturally, it was Leen.

Standing next to her was a stuffed bear, equally excited and dancing around like a maniac.

"We will now dine upon the delicious fruit of forbidden knowledge! Ancient history once unknown! It's all mine now, mine, I tell you!"

バビロン図書館

The Library of Babylon

"...I know you're getting excited and all, but I need to tell you that I'm putting a temporary ban on reading books from the Library."

"What in the blazes did you just say?!" Leen stared at me, fire blazing in her eyes.

We were currently in Brunhild castle. I hadn't yet taken anyone to the Library. I had decided to bring Leen (and Paula, apparently) to my audience room. I broke the news about my discovery there and then.

"I need to think about this pragmatically. You're an ambassador from Mismede. It'd be irresponsible for me to give you untold ancient knowledge. Plus, what exactly are you going to offer me?"

"Oh, so that's how it is... Well, I can understand that reasoning, so... Let me make a proposition. I'd like to become the Court Magician of Brunhild."

"Eh?" *Wait, what? I mean I guess our country doesn't have a court magician, but... Hm. I mean... she's the Matriarch of the fairies, so her ability is definitely high...*

*But she's an ambassador from Mismede, I feel like that'd complicate things. She's a clan matriarch and an influential figure from a foreign nation.*

"It won't be an issue. It's true I'm Clan Matriarch to the fairies, but that's more an honorary title than anything else. Eris is the one who actually handles most of the work back in Mismede."

"Eris?"

"Mismede's court magician. I was thinking of handing clan matriarch status to her anyway, so this is fine. I'd like to retire and devote myself entirely to the pursuit of knowledge." *Hmph... If it's an honorary title then I guess it'll be fine... Not like I'm stealing state secrets or anything.*

I doubted that the Beastking would care, either. He wanted Demi-Humans to be more respected the world over, so taking one as my court magician would do good for public relations. Honestly, there probably wouldn't have been any issues.

"Hm... I shan't be rude. This obviously isn't enough to convince you. I promise to use any knowledge I find in the Library for the good of Brunhild. And, to sweeten the pot, I'll become your wife as well."

"Nope, no thanks. Actually, come to think of it... Are you not married yet, Leen?"

"Incredibly deft dodge of a rare confession, Touya... You won't even consider it?" She was complaining, but I wasn't going to entertain her nonsense. She'd been alive for six-hundred or so years, so I was sure she'd have been married at least once. I wouldn't have been surprised to learn she had kids. "I've never been married, nor have I given birth. Like I said, the growth of a fairy body stops between late teens and early twenties. I was a bit of an early bloomer... As a result, I haven't really been considered marriage material. I get unusual propositions from dubious men now and then, but I've my pride. I won't bow to their fetishes." That made sense enough. Leen would look the same until she died. Not to mention the Clan Matriarch would have to think carefully about choosing a partner.

There was an old saying about pursuing an older woman until your shoes wear out, but... I wasn't quite so sure I was that keen on the idea.

"...Do you dislike older women?"

Leen looked up at me with a somewhat cute expression.

"Ah, well... No. Not in your case, I suppose, but, I mean... You don't feel all that older to me. But as far as marriage goes, it's a whole other ballgame. I do trust you, Leen, and I like you a lot, but... Well..."

"Hm? I find you quite satisfactory, though. I'd be more than happy to marry you. Didn't you notice? I like you a lot, Touya..." *Gah! D-Don't say something like that...!*

Leen jumped up and peered right into my eyes. There was chaos behind her gaze. Mischief. I couldn't look away. I felt like a little frog, mesmerized by a predatory snake.

Just as I was about to comment on her closeness, I felt a little kiss.

"Gh!?"

"Hehe... You've gotten all scared, like a little baby... You have seven fiancées, don't you? You should be used to little gestures like that." Despite her youthful looks, she definitely had a kind of charm that could only come from years of experience...

*This is dangerous. My face is getting red, this is really bad... If she was a stranger, I wouldn't be feeling so conflicted, but... She's Leen! I know her, this is really weird and awkward!*

As I stood there, frozen, unable to think of any way to retort, Leen smiled. "You don't have to give me an answer right away. If it suits you, I'll be quite fine as your mistress or on-the-side lover... But I would like to get married at least once in my life. You'll find I'm quite the devoted type, you know..." She drew back entirely, but not before pecking me on the cheek. *Gh... That's dangerously cute. I almost forgot you're like six-hundred or something...*

"So then, darling... I can use the Library at my discretion if I'm your wife, yes?"

"That was your goal all along, wasn't it?!"

"Well, not entirely... I wasn't lying about liking you, promise. Did you think I wasn't telling the truth?"

"H-Hey now, that's enough… You can look around the Library. But don't share anything that you learn in there."

"Thank you, darling… I love you." *Suspicious… Wait. Crap. Did she just trick me? Did I get seduced?! … No, let's just say that I successfully recruited a powerful ally. Even if I was totally just tricked right now, it's better if I justify it like this.*

As I sighed softly, mulling over complicated matters in my head, Paula slowly shook her head as if to say "Goodness me." *Hmph…*

"Ooh…"

"Wow…" Leen and Hilde let out their surprise as they stepped into the Library. The others were amazed too, but not quite as much.

Leen was astounded by the Library and its shelves, but Hilde was more surprised by Babylon itself. It was her first trip up there, after all.

"How can this be?! I-It flies in the sky…?! Incredible! Amazing! Are there Frame Gears, too?!"

"Be silent. This is a Library. Silence in the Library, please."

"Oh… Sorry." Hilde spoke up loudly, only to be shut down immediately by Fam, who was relaxing on a nearby couch, nose heavily stuck into a book. She was currently reading books I'd had delivered from Moon Reader. Though I did make sure none of the more… unsavory titles arrived in this place.

"Oh, how am I supposed to get a book from the top shelf? Is there a step-ladder?"

"Oh, just touch the shelf and picture the shelf you need." Leen touched the shelf as instructed, and one of the rows of books slowly sank down within reach.

"Amazing… So it can do that, eh? Wait, this book…!" Leen's eyes went wide as she snatched one of the books up. I couldn't read the title, and I assumed Leen couldn't either. Regardless, she began furiously flipping through the pages.

"What kind of book is this?"

"It's an encyclopedia of ancient magic! It's written in ancient magical tongue, but I can read that... Sort of! Can't you see how amazing this is?! It has entries not only on modern magic, but magic that was lost to time!"

"This is a Library. Shh."

"Ah, sorry..." Fam gave out another warning. She didn't even look up from her book. It was a little rude of her, but at least she was enjoying her literature.

"The number of books here is incredible, it is... Would it not be difficult to find a book here?"

"Nope, that's fine, watch. Library... search for books about swords." In response to my words, an arrow rose up to the surface of the red carpet. Now all we had to do was follow it and we'd reach the book we wanted.

Also, putting a book back on any shelf brought it back to its proper position. Basically, there was an automated sorting service. It was plenty convenient.

Yumina pulled out several books and started flipping through them before promptly discarding them. I wondered if she was trying to make Fam mad.

"These books are written in a language most of us can't read... We'll have to have Touya create reading glasses for us."

"Making them isn't an issue. I just need to know what languages to tune them to. Little help, Fam?" I called out to Fam and she rose her head. The girl toddled over to me. I was her master, after all; she couldn't refuse my bidding.

41

Incidentally, I had given her a selection of clothing from Zanac, just like I had with Cesca and the others. I didn't know why she ended up choosing a sailor-style school uniform, but it was simply a matter of taste. She looked like a very studious girl.

"What languages are available here?"

"We have books available in ancient magic tongue, ancient spirit script, Parthenese, Remilia's hidden lettering, Divine Lastian, Godspeak, Deigarese Blabbermouth, Lorad frontsmanese, the gospel, Esteba hieroglyphics, Abanese, Karnar language, Markur, Salieri Tradespeak, Urdenian, Gazur lettering, the tongue of the Continental Fiends, and… I don't recall any other books in any other languages. I've read everything here, after all." *That's insane! But I guess compared to the languages back on Earth, we have more. This world's a little more united than the world I come from.*

If I recalled correctly, the Doctor was from Partheno, an ancient magical kingdom that ruled half of the continent. With that in mind, it was easy to see why most of the books were written in Parthenese.

It was a kingdom that flourished around five-thousand years ago. But it was ravaged by the Phrase. *Oh, there's an idea.*

"Show me books related to the Phrase." I tried searching as a test, and an arrow appeared on the carpet. That was easy.

The country was devastated, but the survivors surely must've written something.

I followed the arrow and made my way towards the designated shelf. I took out a book, which was slightly protruding from the row. Then I invoked [**Reading**] so I could understand the ancient tongue of the Partheno people. Thus, the book's title was visible to me.

"The Magic Crystals." I skimmed through the contents of the book. It mentioned how they hunted humans, discussed their weak points, talked about their ability to regenerate and absorb magic, but ultimately it was nothing Ende hadn't already told me. There was no mention of the Sovereign Core or the fact that they came from another world, though.

It talked about villages, towns, and even cities ravaged by the Phrase, but the information was largely useless to me. It seemed that the Phrase had simply vanished from the world before a real solution could be found. All they left behind was carnage and destruction, so really that's all that could be recorded.

The Phrase had annihilated mankind. Humans, Demi-Humans, and Demonkin alike... Many nations lost their capitals, and the great leaders of the world were all mostly killed as well.

There were a lot of recorded accounts about the last stands of great heroes, but none of it contained new information I could use to my advantage. The authors had simply regarded the Phrase as mysterious magical beings. It made sense, really.

"Oh my..." I reached the end of the book, and found several illustrations. Each known kind of Phrase was drawn, with a little black star next to it denoting its strength, size, and speed.

Just as I'd expected, they hadn't sat around doing nothing. They really were working on ways to prevent the catastrophe.

The types that Ende had called Lesser Constructs were here. I could see a cricket, a snake, a beetle, a mantis, an ostrich, and various other little ones. There was a lot of variety in their forms, but they were certainly the easiest to slaughter.

I flipped a bit further and saw sketches of the Intermediate Constructs. The images were numerous too... there was a manta ray, spider, shark, dog, dragonfly, ladybird, and so on. I'd noticed a few sketches of types I'd never seen. I wondered if the ancient civilization had managed to counteract them efficiently.

They were more easily killed with powerful indirect spells. They were still massive, though. A Frame Gear was necessary to kill them without collateral damage.

Next came the Upper Constructs. I saw a sketch of the crocodile-like one I'd fought, but also ones that looked like a pterodactyl, a hedgehog, a boar, and a few others. If they were all as tough as the crocodile one, then these things were no small matter. Going up against these things with anything less than monstrous firepower would simply be suicide.

I turned over the page once more. The sketch I saw had me reeling in shock. I gasped in horror, and muttered slowly.

"What... Is this...?" Next to the sketch was a single annotation. "Humanoid Construct." The sketched individuals looked just like normal people, with the exception of tiny crystal protrusions on various parts of their bodies. When I checked their statistics, they were listed as considerably stronger than Upper Constructs.

"...I had no idea..." I figured they should be called Human Phrase or something. According to the book, they appeared rarely and were recognized as the most powerful beings ever seen in the world.

I had no idea how many were out there. But I could smell the danger. I needed to improve our defenses, and fast.

Concerned, but determined, I closed the book.

**"Come forth, Fire! Exploding Barrage: [Flare Burst]!"** Linze spoke the words, and immediately five locations in the distance burst into flames. Everything there was annihilated.

This new spell was an enhanced version of [**Explosion**] or perhaps it would be more appropriate to say it was the original version of the spell. It was definitely something else... I was pleased we'd decided to head out to test it in the plains instead of the training field.

"You did it! Hmm... I wonder if Fire suits you better than Water after all, Linze."

"W-Well... I didn't do this all on my own, you know...? Leen is the one I have to thank for getting me this far."

"I'll have you know that fire is my worst element. It's not exclusive to myself, either. All members of the fairy clan share the same weakness. Only a small number of our people can actually make use of it. It might have something to do with us historically being a species that dwelled in the forest." *Hmm... That reminds me, doesn't Leen have six elemental affinities? If I remember right, the only one she can't use is dark. She said something about making Paula to make up for being unable to use summoning magic.*

Paula stood triumphant with her hands on her hips as the explosions sounded off once more... She definitely didn't seem like much of a substitute for someone like Kohaku, though.

45

"Leen, have you memorized any ancient spell variants?"

"That I have. Though mine's from the water pool." Leen stood in front of Linze, extended both arms in front of her body, and focused as hard as she could.

**"Come forth, Water! Raging Whirlpool: [Maelstrom]!"** An enormous whirling tornado of water appeared, rending the ground and eating up the soil. It didn't have any specific target, but it seemed to be some kind of large-scale destructive spell anyway. It was insanely strong, just like the fire one...

"The downside is how rapidly it drains my magic reserves. Still, given what it does, that's only fair." It made sense that stronger spells sapped magic quickly. That was why a good mage knew how to adapt and use the necessary spells for the necessary situation. They had to also take into account just how much magical energy they possessed.

It wasn't just Leen and Linze who had improved their skills thanks to some light reading... Monica and Rosetta had taken in a lot of information on magi-technology, so they were trying some new experiments as well. Some of the books in there were even by Doctor Babylon herself.

Recently, Leen had actually been teaching Sue a bit of magic. Sue only had the affinity for light spells, but her magical power was apparently quite high. Leen had decided to teach her restoration magic primarily, and Sue had been practicing it on the knights after they came back from training.

But she was still doing her maid training with Lapis and the others... I really had no idea what kind of career that girl was hoping to pursue.

Fam had come down to the surface and quickly hidden herself away in the castle library. She was definitely a bookworm and a half... Even book-crazy people I'd heard of back home couldn't hold a candle to her. She'd been indulging for about five thousand years, too, so it was a condition that had spread across her entire body. Simply put, her book-oriented affliction was incurable.

In the afternoon, I headed off to the guild. I decided to pop in at least once a week.

I even accepted a few quests now and then to keep myself busy, but my main order of business was acquiring information from Guildmaster Relisha.

I wore a cowl in the guild, trying to conceal my identity. Honestly, I was sure people knew who I was even with the hood on my head… Still, it was better not to stand out.

"Bastard! You wanna fight?!"

"Bring it on, punk!" Two men had grabbed each other by the collar, and quickly sidestepped outside.

*Again…? Seems like there's a fight every time I come out here. Well, I guess that's just part of guild life…*

Adventurers always wanted to prove their worth, so this was only natural. As long as they sorted it out themselves and didn't trouble the townspeople, I let them take care of it.

"Good day."

"Ah! Your H— I mean, er, Touya… Good day." I was talking to the cat-eared receptionist. If I recalled correctly, her name was Misha. Her cat ears were twitching to and fro, which was pretty cute.

"How's the guild been lately?"

"Let me think… Well, there are a lot of general quests going around. We get the occasional escort mission as well. Still, making a large profit isn't really possible considering the small scale of the quests we have. Some people have been irritated by it, and mostly leave after doing a few missions. Nobody hangs around, so it's mostly an influx of new faces every day." As she spoke, her eyes shifted toward the two men fighting outside. *I see how it is...*

For whatever reason, a lot of newbies tended to think they had to act all macho. They probably didn't want to be underestimated or looked down on, but naturally this was a major cause of conflict, since there were too many people measuring their egos.

It would've been fine if those people were just beginners, but there were a lot of people who couldn't advance to the higher ranks thanks to the lack of quest diversity, so you mostly just had a bunch of tense people hitting each other before moving on.

It'd be a lot better if we had veteran adventurers hanging around to keep things in check... But I couldn't expect people to hang around to get that far if we didn't have anything to offer them.

Misha took me up to the second floor, and I entered Relisha's quarters. The elven guildmaster was clearing up some papers as I entered the room. However, the moment she noticed me, she immediately motioned toward a nearby couch.

"Good to see you. You arrived at just the right time, actually."

"Oh?" She set the papers down on her desk, grabbed one document, and then sat down next to me on the couch.

"I have two pieces of news, and one proposition. Firstly, Dragons have been sighted."

"Dragons?"

"One has appeared south of the Sea of Trees, in the Burning Kingdom of Sandora. From what I've been told it caused chaos in a small sand village, and then flew off to parts unknown. That was fairly standard, but then we heard reports out of Yulong and Roadmare that Dragons were attacking villages in the area. Three Dragons, to be precise." *That's odd... Dragons tend to live up in the mountains away from society, and they rarely attack human territories. Even amongst Dragons, there are elders and juniors. From what I understand, it's the younger Dragons that behave more like wild animals and attack things recklessly.*

Back in Mismede there was that Black Dragon, and it was a younger one. The Red Dragon I met afterward was older, and it seemed like a much more reasonable guy.

"It may be coincidental, but it's hard to say. There's a lot we do not know about dragonkind. It could be mating season for them, or some other migrational event. We're going to proceed with an investigation regardless. Now, on to the second matter... Well, that comes alongside a proposition." Relisha spread out the document on the table, revealing it to be a map. It looked mostly like the ocean, but there were islands dotted here and there.

"This is a recently discovered archipelago south of Sandora. We've found several ancient ruins on these islands, but there's an issue... It's a far-off location, so excavation and exploration are extremely difficult."

"Have you been using ships?"

"Yes, but the islands aren't suited for extended stays. The environment fluctuates to the extreme, burning temperatures quickly become glacial in a matter of minutes. The wildlife there is also beyond dangerous. I wondered why each island had little ruins on it, but it's possible that it was all one large island during the ancient era."

*Hm... A sunken island? That's certainly not impossible. It might even be why they're no longer inhabited. Then the monsters settled in and the rest is history... I guess.*

"The other issue is that the ruins are dungeons of considerable size. We're speculating that they're man-made constructions, likely created by ancient mages or individuals of considerable influence.

If that's the case, it's safe to assume that there's treasure within the dungeons. Naturally the guild can't miss an opportunity to plunder the ruins of old."

*That's definitely true. There could be a whole mountain of treasure down there. I've never personally gone dungeon diving, but as I understand it, there are a lot of ruins scattered across the world.*

"Usually we put out quest notices for cases like this, since it's pretty much the norm for dungeon exploration. However, the location of the ruins poses somewhat of an issue… And that's where my proposition comes in." Relisha leaned in a little closer toward me.

*Wh-What the… P-Personal space, lady…? Though I guess having a woman like this press up against me isn't the worst thing in the world.*

"I was wondering if it would be possible for you to connect those dungeons to Brunhild using one of those [Gate] spells of yours, Your Highness."

"Huh?" *What? Why would I connect Brunhild to a series of dangerous dungeons?*

"What I'm trying to say is that I'd like a way for our adventurers to easily access and challenge the dungeons. If adventurers gather here to explore previously uncharted territory, then the town will develop as well. The guild's understanding of the dungeon will also develop as we send more adventurers there, and we'll all profit from whatever ends up being brought back. What do you think?"

*Oh… That's definitely a good idea.* If I did something like that, we'd have a ton of adventurers coming through looking for a way to earn a quick buck, which would increase business at our inns and shops in turn. Plus, more people being here would end up attracting even more people. I couldn't think of a downside.

I could easily make it so any of the creatures on the other side wouldn't be able to come through the portal, either. In other words, we'd use the dungeon access as a way to promote Brunhild.

"I have a couple of questions, okay? First of all, are the islands owned by any nation?"

"They're currently under the guild's provisional watch, and aren't affiliated with any nation, no. However, if you accept this proposal... I think it wouldn't be unreasonable to have the land granted to the Duchy of Brunhild. Well, that is if you can promise that the guild will have exclusive rights to excavated treasures and any information of worth uncovered."

"Alright, then. Another question. Did you not consider that I might go and explore these dungeons personally? I'd easily be able to monopolize treasure and noteworthy information that way."

"Heheh... I don't believe that a man who gathered the leaders of the world to oppose the Phrase threat would ever do such an awful thing. I didn't get this job just for my pretty looks, you know? I have an eye for judging character."

*Huh. Guess she thinks pretty highly of me. Well, better not let her down...*

It was certainly an interesting prospect. It wasn't going to be me who'd explore the whole place, but the adventurers, merchants, and guild affiliates who had a stake in checking the place out instead.

Even exploring it casually and mapping it out would be profitable. I wouldn't be surprised to find cartographers joining the expeditions, too.

The deeper the dungeon, the stronger the monsters, as well. From what I understood, the density of magic in the air was thicker the deeper down you traveled, which was why the stronger magical beasts preferred to hide underground.

Still, any adventurer worth his salt would be aware of the risks, so I decided not to fret too much about people hurting themselves.

"Very well, then. I'll co-operate."

"Thank you so much! We'd like you to put the [Gate] to the dungeons near the guild, on the outskirts of town."

And so, we'd acquired a new attraction, which was a series of dungeons. With any luck, the town would prosper further as a result. I decided I'd do a little bit of preemptive exploration.

After I had Relisha tell me the location of the islands, I opened up a [Gate] to the Rabbi Desert, which was just outside Sandora. Then, I activated [Fly] and headed off south.

After flying for a while, I finally came across the islands. They were as remote as she made them out to be. Even a ship directly from Sandora would take a long time to arrive.

"Hm… There should be three, right?" Each island had a different dungeon, and there were three in total. I was asked to name them, but I put it off. I was hoping for a flash of inspiration.

"Oho?" I looked down at the islands and saw a ship off the coast. Looking closer, I saw a group camping on the beach of one of the islands. I assumed they were the guild officials who were keeping an eye on the islands. I landed in the camp, and the surprised men drew their weapons.

"Wh-Who are you!?"

"I'm following up on a request from Guildmaster Relisha. Right now I guess I'm an adventurer, so… here's my card."

"Wha— Gold?! Then you must be Brunhild's… Forgive us, sir!" The guild officials immediately sheathed their weapons. The power of the Guild Card sure was something. It seemed like it couldn't be forged, so the credibility of a Guild Card was absolute. Still, I wondered if it'd be possible to fool a guild official with a convincing enough fake...

"Relisha asked me to connect these islands with Brunhild... Hm, maybe I should just bring her here." I opened up a [Gate] and pulled Relisha through.

"...That's certainly what I proposed, yes, but I can't believe you got here so quickly..." I left the talking to Relisha, and she told the guild officials that their jobs were formally over.

These islands were now the extended territory of Brunhild... They were pretty barren, though. It was simply rocky mountains, sandy beaches, blue skies, and restless jungle.

"So then, where's the dungeon?"

"Go straight through the jungle and you'll come to a mountainside. Scale it a little and you'll come to a cave. There, you'll find rocky stairs leading downward. That's the dungeon entrance. This island has a lot of sandy beach around it, so a lot of it's submerged, but it's also very narrow. The dungeon likely goes beneath sea level and connects to the dungeons on the other islands." If it was true that this place used to be one big island, it would make sense that the dungeons connected somehow. There was only one way to find out for sure, though.

"I'll try going in for now, but what about the others?"

"I'll take care of the proceedings back in Brunhild, if you could send me back. Ah, sorry, but would you mind also sending the other guild staff back to Sandora?" That wasn't an issue at all. I quickly sent Relisha back to Brunhild.

After that, the others took down their camp and boarded their ship. They all seemed pretty happy to be leaving. I could imagine

IN ANOTHER WORLD WITH MY SMARTPHONE

that sitting around waiting for orders was probably dull. I could empathize with that.

Once everyone was aboard, I transferred the ship to Sandora's main harbor. That was that.

Now came the fun part, checking out the dungeon.

I decided to head there on foot. It'd be easier to fly, but I took advantage of the walk to chop down trees and create a paved road using Earth magic.

I was attacked by a six-legged wolf and a two-headed snake, but they were small fry and didn't take much effort to kill.

Eventually, I came out of the jungle and made a smooth path up the rocky mountain. Then, I carved stairs into the cliff face to complete the route to the dungeon.

Once there, I entered the cave and looked down the steps into the abyss.

"…Man, that's dark. Not too surprising, though." I cast [**Light Orb**] and generated a little sphere of light. The dungeon felt dank and claustrophobic as I went further down inside. Still, I was probably below the sea, so humidity was natural.

After wandering for a while, I found myself in a broad room. The place was definitely man-made. I could tell from how unnaturally carved the walls and ceiling were.

I looked around and found three different paths. Left, right, and straight ahead. *Come on now… A three-way split in the first room? If this was a game, it wouldn't be nearly this complicated… But I guess it isn't a game, so I should just stop worrying about it.*

I didn't want to get lost, so I went straight ahead. Obviously it was impossible for me to get lost since I had access to [**Gate**] and all.

I traveled on ahead until I reached another fork in the road. This time it was a case of right or left.

*Hm... Guess it's my own fault for thinking the path ahead would just be straight. Wait a second...*

"This might not work, but... display map. Display the first basement floor of this dungeon, and my current location."

"Displaying." My smartphone replied, and it projected a map of the current floor alongside my current position. *It worked... Wow, it seriously worked! Wait, crap... I didn't want that to work.*

It showed the stairs that led to the second floor, too. There appeared to be four floors in total.

*Ugh... I kinda spoiled it for myself, didn't I? I can probably profit by selling this map, but... I won't. It'd be better for adventurers to uncover the secrets of this place by themselves without me spoiling all the fun. Plus, it'd be way cooler to watch them explore this place, like an amusement park. Well, whatever... Guess I can still explore the first floor, at least.*

"Whoa!" I turned toward the passageway leading to the second floor's stairway, and found myself face to face with some monsters. They were short, dog-headed creatures known as Kobolds, and there were two of them in total.

Kobolds were instinctive monsters that didn't understand my words. Other creatures like Werewolves or Vampires did, however.

The Kobolds were expecting me, apparently. At least it seemed that way from their expert timing as they brought their stone axes down toward my head. I quickly pulled out Brunhild and took them both out. Luckily for them, I'd had paralysis bullets loaded. They'd very narrowly escaped a painful end.

I realized that my orb of light was probably an easy way to tell I was coming. It was practically a beacon saying "ambush me" or something along those lines. I should've considered that, really.

I passed the collapsed Kobolds and began heading toward the stairs. I stopped myself for a moment when I discovered a small side passage with a set of double doors at the far end. I made the decision to check it out. Nothing wrong with a detour, after all.

I headed down the passage and opened up both of the doors at the end. There, I found a small room with a treasure chest in the corner. That kind of thing was pretty standard in video games, but it felt a little bit weird to see in reality.

I kind of wanted to ask why there was a treasure chest in a place like this, but I just decided to open it instead.

My heart beat faster as I approached the container, and... I paused for a moment, briefly fearing a trap. I didn't want to blow up or something. I decided to just lift the lid a little bit, so as to not tempt fate. It wasn't locked, at any rate. Anyway, I flung the lid open, wincing slightly, but no trap was set! Upon peering into the open chest, I saw...

"What the..." A rusted knife, a filthy satchel, some wonky looking polearm, and a hand-crafted stone axe. The axe looked like the same kind that the Kobolds from before were wielding. It seemed that I'd stumbled upon their secret stash of junk. Well, it was trash to me, but probably treasure to them. Still, there was no way the guild would want to buy this kind of crap. I took a closer look and saw something gleaming in the corner of the chest. What I saw was a small band of gold. It didn't have any jewels embedded in it, but it was a golden ring for sure. If it was real, it'd definitely be worth something.

...*Come to think of it, where'd they even get the treasure chest?* It was possible that the chest had contained treasure at one point, but the monsters might've taken things from it one by one... Before long, it was simply another storage container for the Kobolds to make use of.

The treasure chest might have even been from another floor. It was possible that someone, or… something, had dragged it all the way up from a lower floor.

The actual treasure might've been looted by the denizens of the dungeon and hidden away in different hiding places… It was entirely possible that the real treasures were in the possession of monsters now.

I took the ring, but left the rest of the stuff behind. *Good luck, little Kobolds… Plenty of people are gonna come through your home and try to kill you.*

Once I made it down to the second floor, I used [**Gate**] to return to Relisha's office.

"It's an ordinary ring without any particular enchantments… Though, it's definitely gold." *Wow, so it's genuine… Guess that means the dungeons do have treasures in there.*

The goal of any adventurer was to find treasure within ancient ruins and dungeons, and also harvest rare materials from monsters as well. It seemed that there were a lot of dungeon-dwelling creatures that evolved differently, so rare materials were commonplace in the lower levels.

"Might I purchase the ring from you, then?"

"Sure, go ahead. How much is it worth?"

"Let's see here… Given the poor handiwork and the scratched surface… About two silver should do."

*Hm… Two silver coins for one golden ring… That's about a week at an inn. Given that I didn't spend that much time exploring, that seems pretty fair. Then again, I might've just gotten lucky finding this…*

That reminded me, if we had more adventurers coming in, I'd probably need to upgrade our lodgings. The Silver Moon probably didn't have enough rooms available.

"There's another matter, Your Highness. The gates that connect Brunhild and the islands… What are we going to do about the toll?"

"Uh, the toll?"

"Yes, the toll an adventurer has to pay. I think you should at least charge an entry fee… Were you planning on making it free?"

"Hm… I guess one copper is probably enough, right?" She told me that was pretty cheap, but there was always a chance that the adventurer wouldn't make it back. I wanted as many people as possible to make it back safely and use the services available in Brunhild.

Making it free would've been troublesome, since we wouldn't be able to keep track of who was coming and going. I didn't want us to lose track of who went through and never came back, so a fee was best for book-keeping. The Guild Card was the easiest way to monitor that. In the end, the toll wouldn't generate much revenue, but that wasn't really the point anyway.

We'd probably need potions, medicine, weapons, and armor as well… I didn't want to get ahead of myself, but I decided to talk to the town merchants about stocking up for the future. It was possible I might end up needing a master smith to repair weaponry and armor, too.

I was a little excited to see just where this project would take us.

Adventurers by the dozen had begun gathering in Brunhild. Why? Because word had quickly begun to spread about the dungeons.

After all, this was uncharted territory. Uncharted and untouched, due to their isolated location. The allure of treasure was far too much to give up on, so many people had come seeking their fortunes.

Basically, it was a first come first served situation. All the adventurers wanted to be the first to explore the dungeons. I'd named them, by the way, Amaterasu, Tsukuyomi, and Susanoo.

In the past I had deliberately limited the knowledge of my [Gate] spell because I didn't want to be looked at with scrutiny or suspicion. But it seemed that it was pretty well-known as my 'signature' magic at this point. I suppose it was unavoidable; I had ended up using it a lot during the Yulong invasion.

I was already in a position of vast power regardless. I didn't expect anyone to turn on me at this point, so there was no real harm in revealing my wonders. Even if they tried, I'd just put them in their place.

All that considered, the portals that connected Brunhild to the dungeons were just accepted as another matter-of-fact thing related to my power.

The dungeons weren't only vast, they were dangerous. Due to the lack of civilization in the area for so long, the place had become a prime breeding ground for magical beasts. Though the exploration hadn't been going on for too long, it seemed that some parties had already made it as far as the third floor down.

The guild was satisfied, since they were seeing a boost in rare items, valuable raw materials, and treasures.

Initially I was worried about the number of adventurers in town causing a disruption of public order, but it hadn't been as bad as I'd thought. There were still some rough types and troublemakers alongside the fortune-seekers, though.

So even though it wasn't large scale, there was a slow but steady increase in dumbasses who thought they could bother my citizens and harass the shop workers.

I wasn't sure what the standard was in other countries, but I certainly wouldn't be letting them do as they pleased. Anyone caught causing trouble would be dragged off to the Whisper Prison (an enclosed space filled with the constant sound of nails on chalkboard), or the Hellish Aroma Pen (another enclosed space filled with a fraction of a sludge slime's scent). That would give them ample time to reflect on their attitudes.

I'd also built a hospital in town, not just for the sake of the adventurers, mind you. I had several Light magic specialists and doctors stationed there, to take care of injury and disease alike. I also had Flora create several medicines to be used by the people there.

We were charging them at a fair rate, but children with parents who were Brunhild citizens would be treated for free. If you were under thirteen in this world, then you were still a child. I didn't want to exclude them from healthcare just because they or their families couldn't afford it.

Well, I said free, but that just meant it wouldn't cost them any money. Their parents would still have to work for a day or two on national projects to make up for it. Though, if they could afford the cash, they could always just bypass that and pay for the medicine like everyone else.

There were a few stalls lined up alongside the portals, stocked with lamp oil, rope, rations, medicines, bandages, and other adventurer necessities. It seemed each stall had a different specialty. One was selling knives, one compasses, one canteens, and so on.

I walked over to one of the stalls and called out to the merchant. He turned to me.

"Hey there. How're the sales?"

"Ah, not bad at all... I might end up switching careers at this rate!" This man was one of Brunhild's ninjas. In other words, he was an ex-Takeda agent, and a subordinate to Tsubaki.

I had him assigned here to disguise himself as a vendor and keep an eye on the people that came through. I didn't want to seem suspicious by talking to him for too long, so I started picking up items on his stall as I spoke.

"Any issues?"

"Nothing major, no. Though there have been various arguments between parties here and there. Minor things." Treasure-related fights weren't exactly new issues. Individual conflicts were fine, so long as they didn't involve unrelated bystanders.

"When I went to the dungeon, there were only Kobolds on the first level. What's the situation on the deeper floors?"

"Common monsters on the first level include Kobolds, Goblins, Giant Rats, Giant Bats, and Lone-Horned Rabbits. Common monsters on the second level include Hobgoblins, Goblin Archers, Skeletons, and Orcs. As for the third floor... I've heard there are Killer Mantises and Dullahans down there." *Huh, Dullahans? I remember fighting one of those forever ago. It was pretty tough at the time. It might be hard to fight without a dedicated Light magic user, or at least anti-undead weaponry.*

"The monsters in each dungeon seem to be quite varied. Amaterasu seems to have an abundance of magical beasts, while Tsukuyomi has an influx of undead. Susanoo, on the other hand, seems to have more generic types of monsters." Apparently the difference between a regular monster and a magical beast was simply down to the bestial features they had. I don't really know why they bothered making such a distinction. But still, I wondered why the

61

different dungeons seemed to favor different types of monster. It may simply be a case of predatory instinct. Magical beasts even ate each other, so perhaps the other classifications of monsters gravitated away from their main grounds.

I thanked the ninja and headed towards the portal. There were three gates in total now, each leading to the entrance of a different dungeon.

Still, the actual location of the islands was the same in the end. There was nothing stopping someone from swimming over to another beach or building a boat to get to the other places. Most adventurers found it more convenient to just come back through to Brunhild and walk through another [Gate], though.

Even if they had to present their guild card and pay a copper coin, it was still easier than moving from island to island the old-fashioned way.

A single copper coin was enough for a meal in this world, so I figured it was approximately a thousand yen. But if that was the case, then I felt like charging two copper coins per night at the Silver Moon was probably a little cheap. Especially since it included three meals. Still, that meant it was around sixty-thousand yen for a full month. Looking at it that way, it was probably fairly priced. *Hmph...*

Regardless, comparing the currency between this world and my old world was a bit of a fruitless exercise. I decided not to think about it too much.

"Touya-dono!"

"Touya...!"

"Hm? Yae and Hilde? What's up?" I turned around to find a swordswoman combo running toward me. They certainly seemed closer lately, probably because they always sparred together.

"We have agreed to set out and investigate the ruins while training at the same time, we have. Hilde-dono has not had as much experience in combat against the magical beasts as I, she has not."

"Yes! Look, I even got a guild card! Though it's still black… It can't quite compare to yours, Yae." Hilde bashfully held up her guild card. She seemed happy.

Her card was black, the newbie's color. The lowest tier possible… It was a bit funny having the Knight Princess of Lestia regarded as the lowest. Felt like a pretty bad joke. I decided we'd work to fix that. Yae's was red. That was because she'd been adventuring with me for a while.

That being said, rising to red in such a short amount of time was practically unthinkable. Still, I couldn't be that surprised about it. Yae was remarkably powerful, she had been even before she met me.

"What brings you here, Touya-dono?"

"Oh, me? I'm just doing a little security sweep."

"Ah, if you're done would you like to come with us?"

"Oh, sure. Let's go." We went through the gate to Amaterasu, and came out on the pearly white sands.

Don't worry, I paid the fee like everyone else. I didn't want anyone making a fuss about me and my fiancees getting special treatment. It'd make us stand out too much, too. Normally I'd have just used my own [Gate], but I decided to use the opportunity to check that these ones were working alright.

The archipelago was composed of seven islands. Some large, some small. There was no dungeon on the biggest island, though. It was basically just wilderness, ruled by monsters and magical beasts.

There were a lot of plant-themed monsters on that island, so people had to take extra care when looking around the place. It seemed there were still some people who ventured on to the main island regardless, and they sometimes ended up getting hurt. But in the end, that wasn't my concern.

It seemed that the island had unusual herbs, nuts, and berries on it, so there was the occasional guild quest to go and obtain them.

I invoked [Light Orb] as we neared the dungeon's entrance. Amaterasu was the dungeon I'd entered originally, and it seemed there were roughly forty adventurers in there right now. If I assumed a party was made up of four people, that meant there were about ten parties down there.

"There is bound to be conflict with so many groups down there, is there not?"

"Well, it's pretty big down there. Even if they do come across one another, they might just say hi and split off again. They might even trade for supplies. I'm sure they won't get territorial about

65

treasure and stuff just yet." Three Lone-Horned Wolves jumped out and attacked us as we entered the dungeon. Before Yae or I had a chance to react, Hilde leaped to the front of the line and took them all down. She was definitely getting tougher.

"What should I do with these? Aren't these horns valuable?"

"Yeah, but just the horns. Their meat's too tough to eat, and their pelts are too wiry."

"So we can just take the horn and leave the rest?"

"Yeah, just push them up against the sides of the walls so nobody trips on them. I imagine they'll become meals for other magical beasts. If not that, then they'll attract slimes when they start decomposing." Slimes lived in every kind of dungeon, apparently. They attacked people every now and then, but for the most part they were harmless scavengers. They ate and dissolved dungeon garbage, basically.

Corpses and waste products were no exception to this rule, either. As a result, most dungeons stayed fairly clean. Slimes be praised.

Even though slimes operated like living vacuum cleaners, it seemed they avoided the contents of treasure chests. But they also tended to avoid metal in general. If I recalled correctly, sludge slimes actually purified bodies of water that they entered. So it was probably a case of different slimes having different cleaning specialties.

There was a theory going around that slimes were actually man-made creations from the ancient era. It was certainly possible. I had no idea about where slimes originated from, after all. Probably a stupid magician, though. I decided to look it up in the Library later on.

Hilde dragged the Lone-Horned Wolves off to the side and sliced their horns off. The horns wouldn't be worth a lot, but the guild would be more than willing to take them off our hands.

Afterward, Hilde deftly took down Giant Bats, Giant Rats, and plenty of Lone-Horned Rabbits. There were certainly a lot of magical beasts in here, that was for sure. Though we did see the occasional Goblin or Kobold peek its head out.

I decided not to display the map, or even reveal that I had one to the girls. We weren't here to chart the dungeon, after all. Plus it was more fun doing a blind run of the place... Though the girls ended up discovering the stairs to the second floor much faster than I expected.

We descended the stairs and made it to another wide room again. There was a left-hand path and a right-hand path. We decided to proceed towards the right. We made it to another crossroads, and then another.

"That reminds me... We should invest in both a map and a compass. If you get lost, you mightn't be able to get back out." Hilde had a point, most adventurers certainly did do that. I, on the other hand, could afford to be lazy about matters like this. I didn't have to worry about getting lost at all thanks to my **[Gate]** spell.

We casually continued on, until we came to a big pair of double doors. We entered through and found ourselves in a small-ish room. There was a treasure chest in the corner, too. I wondered if this was a monster's secret stash or something.

I was picturing the stereotypical game character invading someone's home and opening all their furniture in search of treasure.

Hilde looked extremely excited. This was, after all, her first ever treasure chest. I, on the other hand, just felt awkward.

The chest contained daggers. Lots and lots of daggers. Some rusted, some just dagger handles. All trash. Just as I'd thought. Nothing valuable at all.

But I had no idea why it was exclusively daggers... Maybe the person or creature that stashed them there was just a fanatic. Then again, certain animals like crows and dogs did like to collect weird stuff.

"How disappointing..."

"There there, Hilde. Real treasures aren't so easily found."

"Hold that thought a moment, Touya-dono. Is this not a silver dagger?" I looked where Yae was pointing and, sure enough, though it was dusty and at the bottom of the chest... There was a dagger of pure silver. It was a simple dagger, not very ornate, but it'd definitely be good enough to sell. Treasure was treasure, after all.

"I don't think it'll sell for a lot, but how about it?"

"No... I'll keep this as a memento. A memory of the day I began adventuring properly." Hilde slipped the blade into a pouch at her waist. Well, if she didn't want to sell it, I wasn't going to stop her.

As Hilde smiled, so too did I.

"There, that oughta do it."

"Wow... You're crazy... But I guess that's the norm by now, huh..." I'd just finished renovating the Silver Moon, so I jumped down from the roof.

There were too many adventurers and too few rooms, so I expanded the first building and constructed a second for good measure.

On top of that, the new building was officially recognized as a guild-affiliated adventurer's inn. In other words, the second branch was partnered with the guild, and built close to the portals so adventurers could easily stay there between dungeon runs.

I'd made some tweaks to the main branch and increased the price of a stay a little bit, so it could be the main place for traders and general travelers. I hadn't increased the price by too much, didn't want people calling us a rip-off. Given what the place provided in terms of amenities, we were more than fairly priced.

"You only came to ask if a few renovations would be okay... I didn't expect you to do all of this in just a few hours. I'm amazed..."

"Yeah... It's really something..." Micah, the proprietor, and Fleur, one of her employees, were staring at the new and improved Silver Moon with wide, awestruck eyes.

"Yep, easy does it. All that's left is deciding how many people to hire."

"Ah, in that case... I actually have a few application letters here. There are a few people from back home in Reflet who expressed a desire to move here." *Friends from back in Reflet, huh... Sounds good to me.* I opened up a [Gate] and took Micah through to the sleepy town of Reflet.

We started speaking with the people Micah had mentioned, and it seemed they were all more than happy to come and work in Brunhild.

Some of them even said they wanted to start working right away, so we sent them off to pack their luggage and come back with us on the return trip. It felt a little like stealing citizens, but hey, they wanted to work.

We had some free time after that, so Micah went to go speak to Dolan, her father. I decided to take a little stroll, since I didn't want to interfere in father-daughter affairs.

I hadn't visited Reflet in a long time, so it was a little nostalgic. As I walked, I thought a bit about Brunhild's future.

"I guess we need to restock on weapons, armor, and adventuring goods... Olba's Brunhild store is probably selling out, too... But still, transporting stuff to and from Brunhild takes a while... Carriages can only go so fast." Olba had an artifact that allowed him to transport smaller goods faster than the other merchants, but it still had its limits.

*I'd given up on the idea originally... But maybe I should make a car after all? No, if I'm gonna make anything it should be a train...*

*But then again... horse-drawn carriages are pretty fast, maybe if I could just increase how much they can carry... Wait. Can't I just apply* [Gravity] *to make the carriages lighter? Yeah, that's a great idea. I can make a multipurpose, lightweight horse carriage. Olba would totally buy that, even if it was pricey. Plus, if I enchanted it with* [Storage] *it'd be able to carry a lot more, too!*

I wondered about possible vehicle variations I could make. It might be possible to make a carriage with defensive enchantments for royals or nobles. Mulling over the idea reminded me that my royal stables had no horses in them. That was because we just used [Gate] to get around, so there was no need.

All that aside, things in Brunhild were looking up. The dungeons were highly successful. Nobody had died yet, but there were a number of injured people coming through daily. Apparently after the first floor, the power of the monsters and magical beasts spiked up considerably. If the adventurers couldn't make the proper call, they'd end up getting pretty badly maimed.

From what I'd heard, Amaterasu had been explored up until the fourth floor. Several parties had acquired some valuable treasures from secluded hoards on that level, too. The rumors were getting around, so the number of fortune-seekers would surely increase again soon.

As I thought to myself, I looked to the left and found myself in front of Zanac's store. That was nostalgic. It was the first store I'd seen upon finding myself in the new world.

It looked a bit different now, though. For starters, it was almost twice its original size. They were selling stuff like school uniforms and bathing suits now, though, so they were probably making a lot of profit from their unusual and exotic designs. I decided to take a look inside.

"Welcome! Welcome to Fashion King Zanac!" I entered the shop and was greeted by a slightly older, smiling girl. ... *I guess it's in her job description to greet people like that...*

This store also had a branch in Brunhild, so I knew full well how gaudy and over-the-top a place it was.

I asked the counter clerk to call Zanac over, and before long the man himself was there before me.

"Ohoho. Well, if it isn't His Highness himself. What brings you to Reflet on this lovely day? A matter of urgency, perhaps?"

"We were just looking for more employees to work at the Silver Moon in Brunhild. I ended up coming over with Micah to talk to some people about it. Now I'm here, since I had some time to kill."

"Oho, I see... Does that mean you might like to place an order for employee uniforms?" *Oh, good point. That totally slipped my mind. Zanac sure is sharp, though. He has the trader's opportunistic eye.*

71

I couldn't decide at the time since I didn't know the sizes of the new workers, so I told Zanac I'd put the order in with the Brunhild branch of his store later on.

"Oh, right. I had a small matter I thought I might ask you about, Your Highness. A noble in Roadmare has put in an order for a dress with an unusual, unique design. If it's no bother to you, I was wondering if you might have any… creative input on dresses that look like no other."

"A unique dress design, huh… Hmm. Can I have some blank paper?" As the clerk ran off to get me some paper, I whipped out my smartphone and started browsing for fancy-looking dresses. I picked out about twenty interesting-looking designs. Then I used [**Drawing**] to print off the designs and handed them over to Zanac.

"Goodness… I've never seen anything quite like this. I'm sure the customer will be satisfied with one of these, thank you!"

"Yeah, I'm pretty sure none of the royal families have any dresses like these. So if it's unique they're after, then they won't get much better." If the noble wanted something one-of-a-kind, they were lucky their order came in at just the right time for me to help.

As I printed out a few designs for matching gloves and shoes, a man suddenly burst through the front door with an excessive amount of presence and strength.

It was Barral, the owner of the Eight Bears weapon shop. That was a surprise. But, before I could even react to the bear of a man's dramatic entrance…

"Z-Zanac! There's a Dragon! A Dragon is attacking Reflet, you need to get out of here!"

"What?!" *A Dragon?!* I stormed out the door and looked up, only to see a green-scaled creature circling overhead.

It had deep red eyes, rugged and rough skin, and spines protruding from its tail. It was about the same size as the Black Dragon I faced back in Mismede.

The only difference was that this Green Dragon had two back legs, and wings fused to the two limbs at the front. Unlike the Black Dragon that I'd fought before, which had four legs and a separate set of wings, this one was visually distinct. It was a Wyvern!

"Groaaargh!" The town descended into panic as the beast let out a terrible roar. It craned its neck and began hurling globs of flame from its mouth.

"Gh…!" I used [**Fly**] to get airborne and, deftly weaving between the flaming projectiles, moved up towards the creature. Then, I held my right arm out.

"[**Absorb**]." The balls of flame dissipated into nothing, flowing into my body as raw magical energy. [**Absorb**] was another of my recent Null magic acquisitions. It turned magical effects into magical energy, and granted it to whoever cast the absorption spell. A Dragon's breath was simply the conversion of magical energy to flames, so naturally it was affected too.

But that was still extremely close. Had any of those blasts hit the town, it would've been a complete catastrophe.

"GRAUUUUUURGH!!" The Wyvern's eyes locked on to me, regarding me with eyes that said "Keep out of my way, pest." *Hey, don't you look at me like that! You're the troublemaker here!*

I accelerated towards the Wyvern and gave it a stern kick in the gut. I also applied a certain magical effect alongside the contact.

"[**Gravity**]." The creature suddenly jerked downwards due to the shift in its own weight, crashing down into the main street. Luckily for me, the place was completely evacuated, and now the beast had no way to escape.

I looked down on the Wyvern with a sneer. It was desperately struggling to fly away, but its body was far too heavy. I invoked [Gravity] on myself to massively increase my own weight and, from a height of several dozen feet, plummeted right down on the pathetic creature. I heard a distinct crunching sound as the creature's backbone splintered and snapped. It was dead.

"Man… What a pain in the ass." Cheers erupted from all sides as I surveyed the twitching draconic corpse. Gradually, once all sense of danger had passed, the townsfolk came and gathered around me.

"Goodness gracious me… Incredible… You killed a Dragon just like that, an airborne one at that… Thank goodness you were visiting today, Your Highness…" Zanac quietly muttered as he eyed the dead Wyvern up and down. Barral just stared in my direction, lost for words. Micah and Dolan ran over from out of the crowd.

"This… Good lord, you've gone and done something insane again. I'm glad the town's okay, but… What are you even gonna do with this?"

"I don't really need it. You can have the meat, Dolan. From what I've heard, Dragon flesh is supposed to be really tasty. Zanac, you can have its hide. If you tan it you should be able to make good jackets and so on. Barral, you can have the bones. They'll make good weapon crafting materials." Everyone nearby gasped in shock at my words, but it was Micah who actually spoke up.

"W-W-Wait a second! You know Dragon materials are top-tier, right?! Are you sure you're fine just giving it away like that?"

"Yeah, like I said, I don't need them. It should help everyone out a bit. I'd be happy if you all took it. You guys were kind to me when I first showed up, after all." I'd only spent a little bit in Reflet, but they were good people. I definitely owed them a debt of gratitude. So if they accepted something like this, it'd help me feel like I was giving back a little.

"Ah, be mindful when you strip the tail, alright? Those barbs look poisonous."

"Oh? Got it. Thanks." After my warning, Dolan began carefully stripping the beast's tail of barbs.

*Still... Why was there a Wyvern here? If it was hungry, there's a bunch of Lone-Horned Wolves in the southern forest... It kinda feels like it was directly targeting this town.*

I'd heard from Relisha that there were eyewitness reports of more Dragon attacks in recent weeks.

Weak Dragons had appeared in Yulong, Sandora, and Roadmare. Wyverns were a Dragon subspecies, but still classed as weak Dragons. I wondered why they were attacking people, though. There surely had to be more to this than met the eye.

"Hm? What's this...?" Dolan raised a brow as he peeled back some scales. He had removed the head, but stopped when he noticed something unusual beneath the skin.

I looked over at what Dolan was fussing about, and found something driven deep into the Dragon's skull.

I pulled it out. It was some kind of pointed object, thirty centimeters in length. It vaguely resembled a skewer, and it was fairly thick. From the looks of things, it had dug through the Dragon's skull and penetrated its brain. I could feel a very faint, but very real pulse of magical power running through the strange device.

"...Don't tell me the Dragon was being controlled with this thing." I looked at the strange stake, frowning a little. The idea occurred to me that this might've been another item that fell out of the Storehouse. The thought troubled me for a while, but I put the object in **[Storage]**. I decided I'd ask Cesca and the others if they

75

recognized it later on. If it was from the Storehouse, they'd surely know about it.

But still, the presence of that thing was troubling in itself. If the Dragon was being manipulated by that artifact, then there was some kind of perpetrator out there. A puppet master potentially pulling the strings of a whole species.

I was worried. Mostly because I felt it in my bones. A dark feeling. A feeling that something, somewhere, was about to endanger a lot of people. Much to my regret, I knew then and there that my feelings weren't wrong. Something terrible was going to happen. I'd have bet my life on it.

"I can say with absolute clarity that this isn't one of Doctor Babylon's creations."

"Seriously, Cesca? It's not from the Storehouse or anything?"

"That is correct." A Wyvern had attacked Reflet. It had a strange needle in its brain, so I decided to show it to Cesca. She immediately shot down my theory. Rosetta then took the needle into her hand, and carefully studied it.

"Sir! This appears to be a Dominant Resonance Needle! Surely the handiwork of Professor Elks, yessir!"

"Uh... Elks?"

"Professor Deborah Elks. In the days of Partheno's glory, she was known as a master of magecraft. Several degrees inferior to our dear Doctor Babylon, however."

*Huh... Guess it never occurred to me that there might be more people like her. Still, I'm glad to know this didn't come from the Storehouse. I feel a little less responsible for this, now. At the end of the day, a tool is only as wicked as its holder, so the one to blame here is obviously whoever stuck this thing inside that Wyvern's head!*

*The Blockbracer, the Drainbracer, and that freaky jewel that made people immortal... They were all wielded by wicked people who ended up being consumed by their desires. The Lestian Holy Sword, on the other hand, was justly wielded by a righteous king who came to be beloved by all those who followed him. It's really just a matter of the person behind the item. Still, even if that's the case... it's not like I'll chew out the Terminal Gynoid at the Storehouse any less. It's her fault for being so negligent to begin with!*

"There's a lot to say about Professor Elks, sir! She held Ma'am Babylon in the lowest of esteems, yessir she did! She made plenty of artifacts, and Ma'am Babylon always said that they were strong, but she always neglected safety features, or imbued them with strange effects that ended up causing trouble for their users! Whenever Professor Elks brought stuff to Ma'am Babylon, she'd tell her that her stuff was interesting, but uninspired!"

"Yes, Doctor Babylon had a tense relationship with Elks. The doctor's creations were always of a far higher quality, much to Elks' chagrin."

*That's probably just how that damn Doctor was, though. She probably got a real kick out of teasing Elks. Kinda reminds me of the case of Akechi Mitsuhide and Oda Nobunaga. A genius and a prodigal up-and-comer aren't really in the same class at all. Babylon probably didn't even regard Elks as an opponent or rival... Must've sucked to be the lesser of the two.*

"So what's with this dominatey resonance needle thing?"

"Ah, yes sir! A Dominant Resonance Needle is an artifact designed to take control of magical beasts, sir! It's filled right up with magic and stabbed right through the skull, then the user can control the affected creature at will! It brings out the greatest potential of the affected creature, but also rapidly diminishes its lifespan. There were also risks associated with harming the user's mind, since it forces a mental link between the two, sir! That's why it was ultimately tossed into the trash!"

*I see... It's strong, but also extremely unsafe. I get it. Anyone that tries to use it would end up taking an incredible burden. Then again, I don't really think Babylon was in a position to judge, considering she made that gross immortality jewel... But wait, does that mean the person who was controlling the Wyvern didn't know what they were doing? Or maybe they're still aware of the risk. Even so, controlling a Dragon is bad. They're supposed to be the strongest things around, so getting a bunch under your control spells danger for sure... If a Red Dragon like the one we met back in Mismede came under this mysterious guy's control... That'd be terrible. Still, I don't think an intelligent creature like that could be so easily influenced, artifact or not.*

"Am I interrupting?"

"Huh? Kougyoku? What's up?" Kougyoku came flying in through a nearby window. After perching herself down on the table, she turned her head toward me.

"If I may be so bold, might I suggest we call upon the Azure Monarch and inquire about matters of a draconic nature?"

*Wait... Azure Monarch? Like... another one of the Four Monarchs? The Azure Dragon of the east, wasn't it? Kohaku rules over beasts, Sango and Kokuyou rule over scaled and aquatic creatures... and Kougyoku is the master of birds, right...? Together they make up the Heavenly Beasts, but I don't think they control magical beasts...*

"Dragons are not actually magical beasts, if we are speaking strictly. They are independent creatures and are all related to the

Azure Monarch. Offshoots of their species include lizards, crocodiles, and so on... But those creatures fall more into the domain of the Black Monarch. At any rate, I thought we might wish to call upon the Azure Monarch if we are opposing Dragons. I also haven't seen their face in quite some time, so it might be a pleasant reunion."

"Lord, I humbly refuse!" Kohaku suddenly charged into the room, slamming the doors open full-force in White Tiger form.

*Come on, man! I told you not to grow to that size in the castle!*

"Lord Touya can absolutely solve this problem without having to call upon that wretch, Kougyoku! My lord, I humbly request you reconsider."

*Whoa, calm down! A-And don't get so close to me in that form with those eyes! You're terrifying right now! Don't eat me!*

"Come now, the Azure Monarch would aid us well, would they not?"

"Ssseemss the little kitty isss sstill on bad termss with Bluey-wuey, hm...? How delightfully desssperate, darling... Hehehehee..." Sango and Kokuyou were quick to follow, gracefully swimming in the air. Suddenly, I understood why Kohaku was freaking out.

"Ghh... I-It's true, but still... Things would be bad if that stupid scalebrain came between us, my lord! They're nothing but a wistful chatterbox, do you understand?! Even remembering the Azure Monarch boils my very blood!" Kohaku reduced in size, but didn't get any less angry. Looked like a kid throwing a huge tantrum, honestly... I was amazed to see Kohaku bring personal feelings into this, especially after usually being so cool and collected.

"The Azure Monarch is wise and rational... A terrible mix for the brash and impulsive Kohaku. The two of them are as water and oil. Though I do think it's more that they find it hard to co-operate, rather than the two of them being on bad terms. They surely recognize the positive attributes that the other holds, and they are both equally stubborn individuals."

"Enough, Kougyoku! The only thing I recognize about that stupid blue idiot is their total inability to read the mood!" Kohaku hopped up on to the table and started yelling at Kougyoku.

*...Alright, that's enough. We're not gonna get anywhere like this.*

"Kohaku, I understand your feelings... but I'm going to try the summoning anyway."

"Nooo!"

"Yes. I'm not going to force you to get along, so you don't have to be friends. But I want to take this chance, so at least tolerate one another. I'll get mad if you two fight, got it?" I headed out to the courtyard, Kohaku quietly followed with tail between legs. There was nobody around, so I started the summoning immediately.

I drew the summoning circle using a spellstone as chalk, and poured dark elemental magic into it.

A black cloud formed and gradually began to thicken. As that happened, we mixed in magic from Kohaku and the three others. With that, the preparation was well and truly complete.

"The ruler of spring, of trees, of the eastern domain and the wide-berth rivers... Heed my call. Appear before me!" In response to my words, the black fog began to swell and then dispersed. In its place was an enormous Azure Dragon. Its scales were like sapphires, its eyes were the deepest of blues. Unlike the Wyvern, it was clearly four-legged, and had magnificent wings protruding from its back. Given its mythological similarities to the legends of my world, I half expected it to be a Chinese-looking Dragon, but it was a more typically western-looking one instead.

"...Hmhm. I did think I felt a sudden burst of nostalgia washing over me. To think it was you... Why have you four called me here, then?" The Azure Dragon spoke in a calming, serene voice. She sort of sounded like a gentle female teacher. Or at least some woman in a position of power.

"It's been some time, Azure Monarch."

"Long time no ssseee, bluey."

"You're looking well, Azure Monarch." Sango, Kokuyou, and Kougyoku greeted the new arrival, but Kohaku turned his head and grumbled quietly.

*Come on... Isn't that a little rude?*

"Hm, well then... It seems there's a quiet voice that won't speak up. But it matters not. I am one that rises above such matters."

"Shut up! You insolent blue lizard! You're not above anything, understand?!"

"Hm? It decided to speak after all? Shame... If you have nothing nice to say, you shouldn't say anything at all."

"What?!"

"Alright you two, settle down." I sighed, picking up mini-Kohaku. The Azure Dragon's eyes were intense, but she didn't move. Eventually, she turned to me and spoke.

"Are you the one that summoned me here, human? Name yourself, if you would."

"I am Mochizuki Touya. I'm the grand duke of this nation."

"Interesting. I might understand the case of Kougyoku here, but I do wonder how you managed to gain the co-operation of the White Tiger and the Black Tortoise duo."

"It'sss not a matter of co-operation. Thisss darling is our lovely massster, undersssstand?"

"......Excuse me?" The Azure Dragon stopped dead in her tracks. She looked at me with wide, curious eyes.

In a flash, she started to exude an intimidating aura. It didn't really affect me very much, but I felt the atmosphere changing. It reminded me of the force I had felt when I'd first summoned Kohaku. Eventually she stopped, and let out a small sigh.

"...To resist my spiritual pressure to this extent... Just what are you, boy?" Before I had a chance to reply to the Azure Dragon, Kohaku suddenly spoke up.

"Why don't you find out for yourself, lizard lips? Our lord here wants to make a contract with you, after all. Don't you want to taste the power that we're obeying for yourself?"

"Hmph... As much as I loathe your prattling, little kitten, I'm certainly curious. Very well. I shall test your abilities, human." I didn't miss the grin forming on Kohaku's face. I could tell the exact outcome the little tiger was hoping for.

It was a bit cramped in the courtyard for anything major to happen, so I drew another summoning circle in the western plains and called out the Azure Monarch.

We decided that we'd face one another in combat. The plains were far enough from town to not bother anyone, and the only people here were the other Heavenly Beasts.

"Alright, this good? You ready?"

"Hmph. I do suppose I am. All I wish is for a measure of your skill, anyway. Do not worry, human. I won't kill you." In response to the Azure Dragon's bold declaration, the spectating Heavenly Beasts burst into laughter.

*Oh man, that's pretty good, actually. Amazing, even...*

"Alright then, let's do it. I'm coming for you. Sure you're prepared?"

"No need for further delay. Come at me, human."

"Alright. I won't hold back, then. [**Accel Boost**]." I kicked off the ground and ran full-pelt toward the Dragon. I didn't want her flying off, after all. I decided to end the battle as quickly as I could.

"Wha—?!"

"[**Gravity**]."

"Gwuagh?!" I touched the Dragon's body and triggered my weight alteration spell. In a matter of seconds, she was pinned to the ground, shuddering violently. My strategy was sound. I simply beat her before she could beat her wings. Easy as pie.

"Guh... Wh-What kind of... m-magic is this...?! How can you... w-wield something of this... level?!"

"Gaahahahaha!!! You really misjudged him, lizard lips! Didn't you think to read the mood? We're all here, we're all materialized, and we're all maintained by our lord's magic. Are you so stupid that you don't realize what that means?"

"Oh...!" The Azure Dragon opened her eyes wide in shock. Kohaku continued to tease her while running circles around her immobilized body. Seemed a little too pleased, in all honesty.

"C-Come to think of it... No, this can't be! To keep all of you materialized in the mortal realm... and I as well...! Just how much magic does this man have?!"

"Huhuhu... Lemme tell you something, scalebrain. Our lord's magic doesn't even go down a little bit even with all of us here. Even if there were hundreds of us, it wouldn't make a difference at all!"

"I-Impossible...!"

"Bwahahaaa! You sure look sorry now! That's the power of our lord! Lord Mochizuki Touya! What was that you were saying about not killing him?! Bwahaha! Idiot, idiot!"

*…I mean, it's true, but… you're being a jerk about it, come on. You shouldn't be grandstanding like you're the one with the power, anyway… I mean, I guess you have got a lot of power yourself, but still!*

"You sseem happy, little tiger… Heheh…"

"Well, your feelings are certainly understandable, Kohaku."

"I think you should calm down a tad. Leave her alone, eh?"

*See? Even the others think you're going a little too far.*

The Azure Dragon seemed frustrated by Kohaku's constant teasing, so she made a further attempt to get up. Slowly, but surely, her knees and tail quaked as she rose to her feet. I was impressed.

But then I applied more weight, and she crumpled again like a wet paper towel.

"G-Gaaah!"

"So, do you give up yet?"

"…Y-Yes, I do… I yield. Let us form a contract, human." As soon as she spoke, I released the bonds of **[Gravity]**. Freed from the crushing weight, the Azure Dragon slowly stood up.

"…It was my mistake for underestimating you. Very well, Mochizuki Touya. Grant unto me a name, and I shall be bound to your service."

"A name… Oh, that's right. Kohaku, Sango, Kokuyou, and Kougyoku are all named for precious stones and minerals, so… let's call you Luli."

"…Luli? I… see."

"Yup. It's a contraction of Lapis Lazuli. It's a precious blue stone, understand?" I'd briefly considered Seigyoku, which meant Sapphire, but it sounded a little too close to Kougyoku for my liking. Luli really was best.

"Very well, from now on, I am Luli."

"Mhm… Welcome aboard. Just don't butt heads with Kohaku too much, alright? I'll get mad at the two of you."

"I shall endure that tiger's presence as best I can, don't worry."

"You?! I'll be the one enduring, lizard lips!" Kohaku immediately snapped back at Luli's snide comment. I had a feeling they'd be a real handful.

Luli suddenly changed into a tiny little Dragon, matching the small appearance of the others. I let out a small sigh as the intense staring match between her and Kohaku persisted.

"Why are you two like this, anyhow?"

"The enmity between women is sssomething natural. Even you'd come to harm if you ssstepped between them."

"Geez… Females sure are scary, summoned beasts or not…" Kokuyou let out a little giggle at my comment, and I nodded my head. But then something clicked in my brain.

*Wait. What did he just say?*

"Uh… Wait, between women? Uh, wait, what gender are you?"

"We're all girlsss, obviousssly."

"Don't lie to him, Kokuyou. You're the only one of us that is male." Sango shot down Kokuyou's remark. But that was a little odd… I understood that Kokuyou was a bit of a feminine guy, but… the others were girls? *No way… I thought Kohaku was a guy this whole time! I didn't even think about the others. I mean, Kohaku's voice is a little high, sure, but… I just figured that was part of the tiger aesthetic!*

*I'll… keep quiet about that for now, I guess. I wonder if Yumina knew the whole time… Yeah, she probably did. I'll ask her later to confirm… At least I know Kohaku's a tiger, and not a lion. I'm not that stupid.*

"There are a lot of different types of Dragon, so it's hard to generalize them." Luli began talking, just as I'd asked her. She told me she couldn't do anything about that dominating needle thing, even if Dragons were being controlled by it.

But she also mentioned that the powerful Dragons, known as Elders, would be able to exert enough will to prevent themselves from falling under its control.

Dragons didn't grow conventionally. Instead, they underwent evolutionary transformations. In the beginning they were Infant Dragons, then Young Dragons, then Adult Dragons, and then they went on to become Elder Dragons. Apparently the stage of power beyond even that was a type known as the Ancient Dragon.

But only certain draconic species can evolve into Elders. Lower-tier creatures such as Wyverns could never reach that level.

The difference in intellect was also pretty vast. Young Dragons, like the one I'd killed back in Mismede, could understand human speech, but they couldn't speak it. The needle would be able to work on any Dragon lower than Elder, meaning only the two highest tiers of power would remain unaffected. That was frightening.

"There aren't a lot of Dragons to begin with, so I'm sure it'll be fine."

"Even Young Dragons are mighty, so it takes much to defeat one. It is for this reason that they do not need to breed as much as you land-dwelling beasts. It is true that they are not numerous, but it would be foolish to leave them be for that reason alone. Is your mind clogged with fur, little cat?"

"Why I oughta…!" Luli and Kohaku began squabbling again, so I ignored them and started to think to myself.

*This is a little concerning... The Wyvern didn't exactly seem like it was being manipulated. It felt like it was moving of its own volition. Still, I guess if it's part of the unintelligent lower caste, it might be more appropriate to say that I thought it was moving on its own instincts.*

"I think I should investigate this a little more. That Red Dragon from Mismede's sanctuary might be able to help." The Red Dragon seemed to be an Elder Dragon, so he probably wouldn't be under anyone's control.

I decided to teleport to Mismede with Luli. Then, I headed to the Dragon's sanctuary with my **[Fly]** spell.

"If I recall, the forest at the base of this mountain is the sanctuary, isn't it?" *If I remember right, that means we should already be there.* Just as I was thinking that, I noticed something in the distance.

I stopped in mid-air. What I saw was an enormous Red Dragon coming toward us. I recognized him immediately as the Red Dragon that had appeared after I defeated the Black Dragon back in Mismede.

Luli, who was flying alongside me, grew to her original size. The Red Dragon and the Azure Dragon both nodded to one another.

"I am here to welcome and congratulate you on your manifestation, o Azure Monarch."

"I was only manifested due to the strife amongst your people, young one. Do you understand why we have come?"

"Yes... Please accept my most profuse of apologies." The Red Dragon bowed his head and closed his eyes. We went down to the ground and began discussing the situation with him.

Apparently Young Dragons had been rampaging recently. What I was told reminded me of the brash behavior of the Black Dragon I'd killed so long ago. From what I understood, Dragons were wise and mighty, but that often transformed and surfaced in the form of arrogance due to their status in the world. Dragons were said to be the apex of natural evolution, after all.

Even though they lived in the safety of the sanctuary, some of the younger Dragons would go out into the world to terrorize humanity.

Even if you could just write it off as a youthful mistake, such outbursts often ended up in catastrophe.

It seemed that no matter what the species, there were always unruly brats who defied their elders. Even so, things were worse now than ever.

I was quickly informed that it all began after I killed the Black Dragon.

"What? I caused this?"

"The Black Dragon you killed was nothing special, even amongst his peers, yet they cried voices of injustice after he was slain. Many of the Young Dragons amongst us rallied for justice, and demanded we retaliate."

"What the hell? He was the one that left the sanctuary and attacked them to begin with!"

"Indeed, and for the most part we agreed that it was a justified killing. Only a portion of the youngsters were rallying and crying. Most said that quarreling with mankind was a mistake. So, the troublesome youth amongst us reluctantly silenced themselves." But the story didn't just end there. Dragons had nests and sanctuaries all over the world. Mismede was but one colony.

One such place was far to the southwest. Past the Sea of Trees and between the Kingdom of Ryle and the Kingdom of Sandora, was a small landmass known as Dragoness Island.

One day, a messenger from Dragoness appeared in the sanctuary. He stated that the Dragon King had made his home on Dragoness, and that all should become his subordinates.

"The Dragon King? I thought Luli was the one that controlled the Dragons."

"That's how it should be, yes. This situation is fairly abnormal, on a whole. I was the one who originally decreed that Dragons not war with humanity, and the species has been following my laws for many years. This is the first time I've ever truly been defied."

"It has been thousands upon thousands of years since you passed from this world, o Lady Azure. Some of the Young Dragons are unaware of you, even." Kohaku and the others, the Heavenly Beasts, only manifested once every few centuries. Right now they were in the world because I had summoned them, which was rather rare. My summoning of Kohaku was purely coincidental, but every time after that I'd called upon the Monarchs specifically.

It seemed that Luli, ruler of Dragons, manifested even less frequently than the others. That made sense though, since Dragons lived long and reproduced infrequently.

"So who's this Dragon King? Is he one of the Ancient Dragons?"

"No, he's a man. A demi-human of the Dragon Clan. He appeared on Dragoness Island, took control of the younglings, and massacred every Elder Dragon living there. Then, the remaining adults were forcibly subdued."

*A demi-human… Then there's no doubt in my mind. This guy used the Dominant Resonance Needle to take control. He probably used the younger Dragons to kill the older ones, since they couldn't be controlled by him.*

"All of our younglings fled to Dragoness Island after hearing rumors of the Dragon King's power. They were tempted by strength and the promise of no longer being bound by the laws of our sanctuary. Some of them returned, even more powerful than we had expected. There are a few that haven't come back yet, but we fear they could begin rampaging around the world at any moment." I'd already seen examples of this in Reflet, and heard about it from Sandora. The Young Dragons were running rampant. They killed indiscriminately, as if it were a game, doing whatever they wanted to innocent people. They were just like that Black Dragon.

"What a miserable story... It has only been a few thousand years. Are my brood truly so weak of heart?"

"I-I'm sorry, Lady Azure... There is little I can say in our defense..."

"Hm... Well, I think I get the gist of it. The Dragon King is calling the shots, but the ones running rampant wanted to hurt people anyway, right? So you won't have a problem if I wipe them all out."

"...A Dragon who discards his pride is no more than a lizard. This is the mantra the Azure Monarch left to us before she passed. Those young ones are no longer our own. Dispose of them as you will."

"Pride easily begets arrogance. These Young Dragons are not my kin, they're simply looking down on the world. I recently was foolish enough to look down on this human, and I paid the price in shame." Luli spoke quietly as she looked over to me. There was a saying that said 'the boughs that bear most hang lowest,' meaning that the ones with the greatest strengths were often the most modest. I didn't think the phrase really applied to the Dragons.

Still, humanity wasn't so foolish. No matter the might of a Dragon, humans could still stand against them. Dragons, unlike the

Phrase, were still affected by spells. A talented wind mage could even bring a Dragon down to the ground.

Even so, the damage done would be immense. Captain Garm of Mismede once told me it took around a hundred soldiers to bring down a rampaging Dragon. I didn't want lives to be lost because of this stupid situation. Still, if there were skilled soldiers or talented mages amongst them, they might have an easier time of it. But you would find less of those people in small towns compared to places like the capital cities.

Maybe if they were lucky they'd have good adventurers at their guilds, but there was no defending everywhere. People with the Dragon Slayer title were awarded it for killing them in a party of five or less. To manage that, you'd need at least five Red adventurers, and they were few and far between.

"...Now I'm just a little confused, though. It sounds like they have a stupid, but legitimate, grudge. So I'm wondering if they're even being mind controlled by the needles..." It seemed like the affected Dragons were just doing whatever they wanted, rather than actually being dominated by a singular entity.

It might have just been that the Dragons were having the needles embedded to draw out the absolute brink of their power... Whether they were aware or not of the needle draining their lifespan was another question entirely, though.

Then again, Dragons lived for thousands of years, so it may have been a trivial trade-off.

"The easiest solution would be to take care of the Dragon King, right? But will killing him actually calm the rampaging Dragons?" It wasn't a case where the Dragons would all die if he died. If anything, they'd escape from his control and probably just go berserk. But still, dominated or not, I'd kill any that threatened humanity, so I guess the order in which I took care of them didn't matter all that much.

"Let's trace the Dragons for now…" I pulled up my map and searched for Dragons. *Whoa, that's a lot! Geez, more than I expected. Even if there aren't as many Dragons as there are humans, that's still a fair amount. Hm… Guess I can narrow it down…* I tried a different approach. Instead of just Dragons, I searched for Dragons with the Dominant Resonance Needle embedded in them.

The Dominant Resonance Needle kind of resembled a marking pin. Since its head was exposed, I'd be able to identify it from the outside if I got a look at a Dragon's head. Thanks to that little detail, I was able to successfully run a search.

Even with the search refined, there were a lot… They were quite spread out across the world, flying around at their own leisure, and naturally there was a concentrated group on Dragoness Island, too.

*Huh? What's that…?*

"Wait a sec…!" A group had flown out from Dragoness Island. It was a fairly big one, as well. Then, I noticed their destination.

"They're on a direct flight path to Brunhild!" *What the hell?! Are they trying to get revenge for the Black Dragon?! But why would they even know about me? How?!*

It clicked in my mind that they were probably informed by the Dragon King. It wouldn't be hard at all to ask around about who the famous Dragonslayer who saved a village in Mismede was, which meant that their goal was incredibly obvious.

"Luli. We're in trouble. We need to get home, now!"

"As you wish."

*Are these stupid Dragons seriously doing this?*

*Fine, then! Bring it! I don't care who you are, Dragon or human or anything else! Nobody attacks my home.*

*I'll crush every last one of you arrogant bastards!*

"So yeah, there's a horde of Dragons on their way here right now. I'll wipe them out though, so don't worry."

"…Baba-dono, I have no idea what to say to this young man right now."

"Well, Yamagata. That makes two of us." I was in the conference room with Yamagata and Baba. Both old men turned to me in sheer shock.

I gathered all the major members of my knight order and briefed them on the situation. I'd gotten back to Brunhild using a [**Gate**], meaning I still had a good lead on the Dragons. Everyone looked at me, unsure what to say. Eventually, however, Nikola broke the silence. He sighed slightly and stood up.

"Y-Your Majesty, please… Uh, well… When you say Dragons, are you referring to the creatures that fly in the sky and breathe fire from their mouths? Those Dragons?"

"Yep, that's the ones. Apparently some of their young ones got all cocky, so now there's a horde of them heading our way."

"A… horde, you say. Just how many?"

"About twenty regular Dragons, give or take. But there are about a hundred lesser Wyverns traveling with them too. Barely anything compared to the Phrase we faced recently, right?"

"W-Wait, wait, wait!" Commander Lain had spoken up to ask about how many Dragons there were, but after I answered, she and Nikola both started freaking out.

"It's gonna be fine, right? Boss-man'll take care of them no problem, like he usually does... Right?" Norn grumbled with mild concern as she spoke up. Her lupine ears were shuddering slightly.

"I thought about it, but then I realized this is a golden opportunity."

"An... opportunity?"

"Yep. What better training exercise could there be for our knight order? These Dragons will make perfect targets, don't you think?"

"Excuse me?!" Lain looked at me in utter disbelief. To be honest, I thought my country's knight order was a thing of beauty. We were strong, but we also lived in a land with few monsters, and we were situated directly between two friendly territories. It would be good for them to get a proper training exercise done.

"O-Our knight order doesn't even have a hundred people in it, and that's including our intel corps! We can hardly pair one person to one Dragon, either! How are we meant to fight airborne enemies, anyway?"

"I'll bring down the airborne ones. After that, you just need to focus on avoiding their deadly breath. You should be able to do it, sort of... I mean, your shields can resist fire!"

"Sort of, huh...?" I'd employed safety measures. I wasn't going to risk their lives, after all. Plus, my fiancees and the Monarchs were to act as backup. I didn't think the Dragons would be pushovers, so that was only natural.

Even if it was a tough fight, it'd be good to do this. We were a newly-established country, so we were likely being regarded by prying eyes. If word spread that our knight order managed to fend off over a hundred Dragons, we probably wouldn't get any trouble from countries like Yulong again.

"W-We'll be able to beat the Dragons easily with the Frame Gears... Right?"

"We won't be employing the Frame Gears for this battle."

"What?!"

*I want to show these arrogant lizards the power of humanity. I'll show them just who it is they decided to judge by their covers. After all, they're attacking us out of some misplaced anger. Let's shove it back in their faces.*

It'd be far too easy a victory if I called out the Frame Gears, anyway. We wouldn't get much in the way of real combat experience. I didn't want my knight order mistaking the power of the Frame Gears as their own power, after all.

"And here's the most important thing of all."

"Hm?"

"We'll be able to harvest the Dragon corpses for rare materials, and profit big-time."

"......"

*Damn right. Leather, bone, horns... If it's draconic, it's worth a lot. One Dragon alone is a fortune in itself, so killing over a hundred is an incredible chance to make a ton of dough.*

"It'd help the country a lot if we had that money."

"......"

"I'd also be able to use the proceeds to pay out a huge bonus to all my hardest workers."

"Booyah!"

"Let's go get those Dragons!!!"

*So easy to manipulate...*


"I see them in the distance. They look about three minutes from arriving." Luli warned me, so I used [**Long Sense**] to see for myself.

There were a lot of Dragons for sure. We were in the southern plains, just outside Brunhild Castle Town, waiting for the Dragons to arrive. We wanted to avoid any real damage to our nation, so we chose a wide open space as the battlefield.

"They're noisy…"

"They're speaking draconic, saying things such as 'kill them all' and 'roast them alive'… A lot of obnoxious laughing, as well. Truly, these beasts are not my kin. They are far too lowly for that. Or perhaps their minds were infested by that cursed artifact…" I didn't speak draconic, so I had Luli translate. I was glad she had such a good sense of hearing. I was a little irritated to hear what they were saying, though… Still, it gave me good cause to go all-out in killing them.

There was no room for discussion here, so I decided to knock the wind out of their sails.

Once you've identified your enemy, defeat them before the battle begins. That's what my grandpa always said.

**"Come forth, o Storm! Million Blades Borne of Air: [Tempest Edge]!"** I invoked an ancient wind spell I'd learned from a book in the Library.

A great storm suddenly appeared, sucking the Dragons into the heart of it. It shredded their wings to pieces.

"GRAUGUUUUUUH!!"

"GUYOOOOOOGH?!" The Dragons, screaming horribly, all tumbled to the ground. If I was being serious, I could've killed them all then and there, but I only wanted to maim them for the time being.

Kougyoku, who had taken her regular phoenix form, cast a rain of fire down upon the grounded Dragons.

"Brunhild Knight Order, chaaarge!!!"

"HOOOAAAAAAH!!!" My knights brandished their crystal swords and shields, charging forth in response to Commander Lain's order.

The Dragons suddenly turned toward them, breathing out a torrent of flame. But suddenly a wall of water appeared between the two forces, massively reducing the heat.

"Tough luck, darlingsss… Try again, hm?"

"We're indeed masters of defense, let us show you." Kokuyou and Sango were in charge of defending against the fire breath. I stood atop Kokuyou's shell, since they were both back in their original forms, and watched as my knight order charged in against the Dragons.

Kohaku was in her original form too, charging toward a group of Wyverns. She roared out, releasing a shockwave that knocked everyone caught up in it backward.

"I'll go as well. I can't leave it all to that fuzzy fool, after all."

"Try your best to support everyone evenly."

"As you wish." Luli spread out her wings, letting out a deafening roar as she took to the skies. Almost in response to it, the Dragons looked over to her and froze. If I had to guess, I'd say she shouted something at them, but I couldn't begin to know what.

Even my translation spell couldn't decipher draconic, probably because it was an animal language. I'd probably need a telepathy spell to understand what they were saying. And to be honest… I bet I could find a spell like that if I looked.

Luli flew off, firing blasts of fire at the clustered Dragons. A few Dragons were blasted off into the distance.

*Hey, that's my money! Don't launch too many too far!*

Luli didn't have anything to say about my plan to sell the corpses either, so I assumed she had really given up on them.

I thought it was a little cold of her, but she just had a very strong survival of the fittest mentality.

"We'll support everyone as well."

"Indeed." Linze and Yumina turned to me before chanting some wide area of effect spells. They'd been doing more reading in the Library than I had.

**"Come forth, Fire! Burning Barrier: [Fire Resist]!"**

**"Come forth, Winds... Blessed be the Updraft: [Tailwind]!"** Everyone in the knight order found themselves engulfed in red and green lights. The two spells had granted them heightened resistance to flames, and increased their agility.

"Tower corps! Front lines! Assault corps, right behind them!"

"Understood!" Ten soldiers with large shields formed a row and tanked the breath of a Dragon. From behind them, several knights wielding crystal spears poked their weapons through the shield gaps, stabbing the beast.

"Gwaruuugh?!" Dragonscale, which was harder than steel, was still no match for phrasium weaponry. The Dragon was more confused than hurt, but not knowing why it was dying wasn't going to save it.

"Haaa!" Lain, using her innate rabbit qualities, leaped over the tower knights and landed on the Dragon. Her crystal sword was plunged right into the Dragon's head, putting an end to its flames.

The Dragon spasmed and convulsed two or three times, then lay still. Lain pulled the sword from the creature, and relayed more orders.

"On to the next one!"

"Aye!"

*Good work, Lain... and good work, knights! Support magic aside, around ten people taking out a Dragon is no less than incredible. Plus, the needle in their brains makes them stronger than Adult Dragons, too. I guess my 'sister' training these guys is finally starting to pay off.*

"Touyaaa… Y'mean I really can't go in too?"

"Moroha. It's not gonna be a training exercise if you go in and wipe them all out in a few seconds, is it?" The God of Swords stood beside me, clearly angry that she couldn't fight. She wanted to fight, but she didn't even have a crystal sword. Her weapon would just get all scuffed up. That being said, I had a feeling she'd just bash all the Dragons to death with her sword's hilt or something… She was that kind of girl.

"You never know, Touya. Could be some kinda worst case scenario situation. Wouldn't it be better if I was in the fray?"

"Ugh… Fine, whatever. You can go over… But only as a support, alright? Just watch! Don't you dare go all-out on them!"

"Ahaha! Fine, whatever! Just give me a sword already!" I sighed, opened [**Storage**], and passed a crystal greatsword over to Moroha.

She merrily skipped over to the Dragons, slicing open the legs of any unlucky beast she passed by. I had just told her not to overdo it, and she was already causing them considerable injury… Still, at least it meant we had no chance of losing. I'd just sent out our most lethal weapon, after all.

"We seriously can't help…?"

"Now that my sister's out there, definitely not. None of the knight order would be able to do anything if you all went out there." Elze, Yae, Lu, and Hilde were all sulking nearby. But my mind was made up, and their grumpy faces wouldn't sway me. Moroha was way, way more than enough.

If I just sent whoever over there, the fight would quickly become a crazy free-for-all. I had Kougyoku giving fire support, Sango and

Kokuyou protecting everyone, and Kohaku and Luli were leading knights to their targets. That was more than enough.

As for me, I was tracking the wounded and fixing them up with recovery magic. Since Sango and Kokuyou were suppressing the fire breath, I couldn't imagine anyone getting injured too badly unless they took a direct hit from a swipe or something.

"Hm?" I saw a Wyvern trying to fly with its tattered wings. It got about ten meters before being socked in the face by one of Kougyoku's fireballs. *Heh. Nice.*

"HAAAH!!!" Old man Baba roared like an animal as he plunged a spear into a Dragon's head. He had crushed it in a single blow.

He was old, so I wanted him in the rear as support... but he completely ignored me and charged into the front lines. Yamagata was nearby, swinging his greatsword at a wyvern as he slashed the heels of a Dragon beside him.

"Hey, hey, hey! Get over here, you scaly twerps! Feel the might of a real man!" The fight had been going on for a while, so things were getting pretty tense.

The two old men refused to board Frame Gears whenever we used them. They had said that they didn't feel like it was a real fight when they piloted them, but they really seemed to enjoy getting up close and putting their lives on the line. I was a person who put safety first, so I didn't really understand their reckless attitudes.

"Fuh!"

"Hiyaaah!" Nikola shook his halberd, and Norn slashed with her twin blades. I had prevented them from bringing in their mounts, and naturally that extended to Lain as well.

I wanted them to see the battlefield from the ground. If they had ridden a Griffin or a Pegasus, they'd have better vantage but poorer defense. They'd be able to deflect the breath attacks with their shields easily, but their mounts would have taken the full hit.

Before I knew it, most of the Dragons were down for the count.

One of the remaining Dragons seemed to be screaming something, but I had no idea what they were trying to say. I asked Kokuyou, who was coiled around Sango's legs.

"What's that one saying?"

"Jussst a tirade of abussse, sssweetheart. It'sss calling you inferior creaturesss, and criticizzing you for attacking them in groupsss. Missserable, if you asssk me."

*Geez... They're the ones that came to attack us in a group in the first place!*

Luli suddenly turned to the wailing Dragon and unleashed a torrent of blue flame that burned it to ashes. *Well, there goes my profit.*

"Little Luli is posssitively furiousss. But that'sss only natural... I too would be enraged if my kin acted in sssuch a manner." Kohaku smacked away a Dragon that was about to bite a member of my knight order, then slashed out its eyes with her claws. After that, she left it unable to fight, but still alive. It was almost as if she was calling it unworthy to face her.

"It'll be over sssoon."

"Are these guys really stronger than Adult Dragons? They seem too weak."

"Perhapsss they're sssimply ssstronger in a cassse of one versssus one, darling. It may be that they aren't any good againssst groupsss. They aren't working in tandem, ssso they're jussst attacking however they like. Great ssstrength hasssn't tempered their weak mindsss. There isssn't a cure for idiocy. If there wasss a single Elder Dragon amongssst all of thessse, they might have had a fighting chance."

Dragons weren't creatures that hunted in groups, so it made sense. They were simply uncoordinatedly attacking like this.

Just as Kokuyou had said, it was pretty much over. The Dragons that remained were being put down one by one.

Eventually, they were all dead. Our side suffered minor injuries at best, as well. It was a complete and utter decisive victory.

"Raise your war cries, victors!"

"HOOORAAAAAAH!!!" A victory cry exploded across the plains.

*Well, we won. I can't help but be a little disappointed at how much of a cakewalk that was, though.*

I hadn't noticed during the fight, but we ended up gathering a crowd of spectators. It wasn't too surprising, since our battle had generated a lot of noise. They were mostly people from town who had come out to see the commotion. I recognized a lot of adventurers from out of town amongst the crowd, too.

"Y-Your Majesty... Just what happened here...?" Guildmaster Relisha ran over to me from out of the crowd. Several guild staff members followed close behind. She briefly glanced at Sango and Kokuyou, fear painted on her face. After a moment she realized who they were, and calmed down a little.

"I went to the castle because we'd gotten word about a horde of Dragons heading toward Brunhild, but you weren't there... Neither were the knights, so I had no idea what to do!"

"Ahaha... Sorry about that. Seems we just missed one another. But don't worry, we took care of it."

"I... can see that, yes." Relisha looked over the field of dead Dragons with a look of awe on her face. I decided that I'd have the adventurers play their part in this little story, too. They'd be able to spread stories to other countries about what had happened this day.

"Yep, we did it well. So, will the guild be able to buy these?"

"Wh— You mean all of them?! I… I mean, we can definitely purchase them, yes… But please let me arrange funds before I buy them all… At a glance, I could probably pay for ten of them using our current Brunhild treasury…"

"That's fine. I'll store the rest of them. For the time being, at least." I invoked [**Storage**] to prevent them from decomposing in the meantime. All that was left was to cut up a few of the dead bodies and cook them. Roasted Dragon meat was supposedly a delicacy, so I wanted to share it with all the people of Brunhild.

I used my smartphone to project an image of myself above all the knights in the field.

"Good work, everyone! You've proven yourself as great knights of Brunhild this day. I'll roast up a bunch of Dragon meat, so eat to your heart's content! And naturally, I'll be putting in a little financial bonus for you all, too."

"Hurray! We did it!"

"Looks like meat's back on the menu, boys!"

"Man, I'm starving…"

"Thank goodness, now I can pay off my gambling debts."

"Brunhild Forever!!!" The knights cheered out in joy. I was happy for them, too.

"Also, we'll all be taking the Frame Gears to Dragoness Island tomorrow. The plan is to exterminate every last Dragon there, so make sure to get a good night's sleep, and I'll see you all in the morning."

"WAIT, WHAT?!" All of the knights looked like deer in headlights. Honestly, it was pretty damn amusing.

Dragoness Island.

It was a little bit smaller than Brunhild was. Dragoness Volcano sat at the center of the island, spewing out ash. For the most part, it was an uninhabitable wasteland.

The Dragons mostly lived on the beaches that lined the island. They tended to eat large fish, or aquatic magical beasts. Occasionally they'd leave the island to hunt game in dense forests, away from civilization.

But things were different now. They'd been attacking farms, making off with livestock, raiding fishing boats, and running rampant.

There wasn't a single Elder Dragon left on Dragoness Island, so there was nobody to keep the young ones in check.

Luli and I arrived on one of the sandy beaches. The moment we arrived, she let out a furious roar that echoed across the entire island. *You trying to burst my eardrums?!* In response to her cries, several screeching roars came back from the distance. Dragons then began to show up in droves. Wyverns, Sea Dragons, Earth Dragons… All kinds of subspecies were on their way to us.

"We're surrounded."

"What'd you say to them just now?"

"I called them lowly beasts that have shed their pride. And then I asked them if they were ready to die."

*Well… I guess that's fair. I did come here to wipe them out, after all. But still… subtlety is a lost art to you, huh?*

"Enough screeching! My ears are gonna give out…!" I had no idea what they were saying, but it was obvious they were protesting her comment. It just sounded like a bunch of crap to me, though.

"Ohoho, goodness gracious! What manner of Dragon tamer is this?" A draconic humanoid walked across the sand, pushing his way past a few Earth Dragons.

The Dragon Clan had a lot of tall, sturdy people in it, and this man was no exception. He was about two meters tall. His armor was beautiful, too, as was the flowing cape coming down his back. He had red hair and golden eyes. He also bore horns and a tail, easily recognized characteristics of a Dragon demi-human.

"I take it you're the Dragon King?"

"Ohoho? I see that word of me is spreading already, lovely. And you are?"

"I'm the grand duke of a small nation known as Brunhild." I saw the man's brow quirk slightly. Seemed he knew just who I was.

"…Ohoh. Welcome to my humble abode, then. You seem to have done well against my subordinates."

"Done well? They were hardly even interesting enemies. By the way, that Dominant Resonance Needle of yours is defective. It's better to throw an artifact like that in the trash."

"Wh—?!" The man adopted a panicked expression on his face. He probably had no idea I knew about his secret, after all.

"So, just in case I'm wrong… let me ask to be sure. You're the one manipulating the Dragons, right?"

"Manipulate? How quaint. I've liberated them from bondage, that's all! From the chains of their elders! From the shackles of their laws! A Dragon is mighty, noble, wise. Why must dragonkind distance themselves from humanity, when they are the apex of evolution?"

"Noble? Wise? Every Dragon here's an ignorant dumbass."

"I concur," added Luli. I was glad she agreed. After all, if they were actually clever, they'd have run away long ago.

So in the end, this guy was exactly what I expected. A racial supremacist. A draconic supremacist. From what I understood, the Dragon Clan of demi-humans was a prideful bunch who went off into the world to hone their own bodies and minds. They forged their own paths.

But as we saw, pride easily turns to arrogance. Just like Dragons themselves, draconic men and women were susceptible to the same pitfalls.

"Didn't those mighty Dragons of yours lose to some puny humans?"

"Silence! It's impossible for a Dragon to lose in a one-on-one battle with a lesser creature! Measly little humans have only one advantage, they breed faster. Like insects, almost. You have no right to talk of us that way!"

"If you're arguing like that, then you could say fertility is humanity's strength, and we should be more than within our rights to fight in numbers. Not that it matters. I could kill all these Dragons by myself." To be fair, I was technically a Demi-God at this point, so it was arguable if you could call me a human... Still, I was still pretty sure Yae or Elze could defeat Dragons alone too, so I wasn't totally off base.

"And you've come to my island for this reason? Impressive, human. You have a lot of guts. But it's misplaced bravado! Do you not see the power I wield? I could take over the entire world! You dare defy me?" The Dragon King yelled at me, but he was sweating profusely. *Really, now? I mean, sure... there are over five-hundred Dragons here and all, but... can you really conquer the world with this much? I don't buy it.*

"Well, how about it? Join forces with me, child, and I shall grant you half of the world. We must—"

"Snrk…."

"What are you laughing at?!"

*How could I not laugh?! You're a dumbass, Dragon King! Who the hell says that kinda cliche crap in real life? I'm not exactly a hero or anything, but my answer is a hard no.*

"Right now your Dragons are just an angry mob, isn't that right? They're a useless gathering of idiots without any direction. Do you want me to tell you what I think, Dragon King? I think you aren't commanding them, you're just drawing out their power and sending them out without any kind of co-ordination. You talk big, saying you can command Dragons at your will, but… I bet you can only control one or two before the strain's too much for your pea-brain to bear, am I right?"

"Guh!!!" *Bullseye. Seems Cesca was right about that needle being a shoddy product. Looks like this guy's relying more on bravado than actual power.*

"Ha… Hahaha… Fool. Why would I need to directly manipulate these ones, anyway? You're an enemy to our kind, Dragon Slayer. All these Dragons here are awaiting my command. I need to say but one simple word, and they will ki— AHGUGUUUHGHAH!!" In a flash, the man's upper body vanished from sight. It was engulfed in the maw of a Black Dragon. And then I heard a crunch.

*Holy SHIT.* His lower body slumped to the ground, trickling blood from its oozing wound. It was disgusting. The beach sand dusted his sticky organs as they splattered out. These Dragons couldn't speak human languages, but they could certainly understand what was being said.

They were arrogant, after all. It was only natural to assume they'd be reluctant to serve under a demi-human, even if he made them stronger. But it seemed like they were going along with him because they thought he could control them at will. However, once they found out the fear was baseless, there was no reason to keep him around anymore. That was the most likely reason for the Black Dragon's actions. The Dragon King had revealed his own fatal flaw.

"Well, I guess he got what was coming to him, but… that doesn't solve the main problem."

"They're already starting to yell things about spilling blood, and killing humans… What a terrible sort…"

"Man, what a pain. Let's take out the trash already." I snapped my fingers, and a [Gate] opened up. A loud series of thuds heralded the arrival of several Frame Gears on the island.

The Dragons turned their attention to the sudden invaders. I could sense their irritation. I'd summoned fifty Frame Gears in total. That was only about a tenth of the number of Dragons here, but I felt it was enough.

"Everyone, listen up. Don't hold back, go all-out. We'll have a Dragon BBQ cookout tonight!"

"Hoorah!!!" I spoke through my radio and informed all the pilots of the plan. This would be a much easier battle than the last. Dragons weren't nearly as strong as the Phrase, and magic worked on them just fine as well.

I was actually more worried about fifty Frame Gears being overkill. If we mashed the Dragons into paste, we wouldn't be able to sell them… Still, we couldn't exactly afford to go easy, either.

Well, it was too late to worry about that anyway. We were fighting for the sake of the humans who had been put at risk, as well as that of the real noble Dragons who wished us no harm, and to also line Brunhild's coffers with bountiful gold. We couldn't afford to hold back. It would be disrespectful to those that had already been victimized.

"Brunhild Knights, charge!"

"HOOOAAAAAAH!!!" At my command, the Chevaliers marched forward. The Dragons unleashed flaming breath and balls of fire, but they were easily shrugged off by shields. In a matter of moments, several Dragons lost their heads.

The Dragons started trying to fly away, apparently having realized the power of the mechs. But it was too late. Several of them released wind magic and brought the airborne creatures crashing to the ground.

The Ether Liquid that fueled the Frame Gears also transmitted magic all over the surface of the mech, allowing spells to be channeled through them. This didn't really work for restoration spells or anything like that, but it allowed them to cast spells while piloting. This was because Ether Liquid held the same properties as spellstones.

The Chevaliers descended upon the fallen Dragons, making quick work of them. I didn't really mind seeing heads fly due to decapitation, or their flesh being pierced by spears... but I had expressly forbidden the use of maces and hammers for this fight. Mulched Dragon meat didn't really sell so good. *Wait, don't trample them! They're valuable, damn it!* The Black Dragon who had eaten the Dragon King (I didn't even catch that guy's name), was restlessly glancing around the battlefield. He watched his comrades die one after the other, and I could feel the fury emanating from him. Luli noticed too, and took a step toward him.

"Luli?"

"Allow me to punish this child. He discarded his pride as a Dragon. I will show him the true power of my kin."

"Uhh... Alright, I guess. I see where you're coming from."

"I am in your debt." Luli turned and let out a deafening roar. If there were any wine glasses nearby I was sure they'd have been broken. *Damn it, my ears!* The Black Dragon roared in response, but compared to Luli its voice was miserable and weak.

I wondered if it understood its predicament, but then it suddenly shook its head and fired a fireball directly at Luli. She tanked the hit, didn't even flinch.

I was a little surprised that she was completely undamaged. Not a single one of her azure scales seemed out of place.

The Black Dragon panicked and took a few steps back. However, it was too late for that. Luli charged forward and took its throat between her jaws. The creaking sound of splintering scale and bone rang out across the beach. *Urgh... That's... I'm gonna puke...*

The dead Dragon fell on to the sand. Luli reared her head, roaring a deafening tone once more.

Suddenly, various Dragons stopped their protests, and fearfully huddled on the ground. A message came through on my radio.

"Your Majesty... Many of the Dragons have stopped fighting...."

"Luli... Is this a surrender?"

"It is. I just told them all to give up if they value their lives. I told them that resistance is futile. I told them that, if they didn't wish to become ash, they would give up in the name of the Azure Monarch."

*You think I'd let you turn them into ashes? They're too valuable for that!*

All jokes aside, it seemed there were a few Dragons among them that knew about the Azure Monarch. But not all of them. There were still some trying to attack.

"Don't fight the Dragons that surrendered. But feel free to kill the ones that are still being aggressive. There's always the chance they might pretend to surrender, so don't let your guard down either."

"Understood!" After a while, we had killed three-hundred-and-fifty of the five-hundred or so that were originally there. Then, we took the needles out of the living and dead ones alike. This artifact was a real pain in my ass, but I was sure we'd gotten all of them. It was possible that back in the old days, they'd been gathered somewhere for disposal, but weren't able to be destroyed for some reason. And then after thousands of years, someone came across them all and figured out what they could do... I did want to know more about the needles, but the only guy who had figured them out was half the man he used to be, so I was out of luck. I buried the Dragon King, or his lower body at least, by the coastline. I also buried the Black Dragon that had killed him nearby. I didn't do it out of some sense of honor or compassion or anything, though... I just didn't want to bring the Black Dragon back and deal with the gross half-corpse in his belly.

If you misuse something powerful, you may fall victim to it in the end. That was the lesson I took from that incident.

*With great power comes great responsibility. If you don't recognize that, you may already be dead.*

"Alright, this is the rest of what you're owed for the Dragon carcasses." Relisha passed a bag over to me, and I promptly opened it up. There were roughly twelve bags, and each had a hundred royal gold coins inside. It brought my total up to a tidy sum of one thousand and two hundred. There was really no point in comparing it to the currency of my old world, but it was about twelve billion yen in total. Not too shabby at all.

Royal gold coins were rarely used in regular transactions. Instead, they were mostly found in matters of national trade or business takeovers. That was because losing one would be disastrous.

I'd received this much solely for the corpses of the Dragons that had attacked Brunhild. The ones from Dragoness Island were still being kept in [**Storage**]. There were around a three hundred and fifty of them in total.

I didn't want to sell them all because it could've had disastrous effects on the economy if I suddenly forced the guild to buy them all up. I knew they'd be able to profit from them, too.

I decided I didn't want this many dead Dragon parts circulating around the world at once, so I left it at that for the time being.

"Rumors are already beginning to spread, you know? They're whispering that Brunhild's knight order massacred an army of rogue Dragons."

"It's a pretty unbelievable story, though. I wonder if people'll end up going along with it."

"Me too. I was there, I saw you all do it… and even I can't believe it. But there's no doubt, word of this country's strength is spreading like wildfire. I'm certain that anyone with ill intent might reconsider their options, now." And that was just what I had wanted. I didn't want a repeat of the Yulong incident, after all.

There were still a bunch of Yulongese people prattling on and on about how I was the great summoner of the Phrase, and how I had orchestrated the destruction of their nation. They keep saying stuff like "Brunhild must atone for their sins" and so on. It was annoying, frankly. I had no intentions of paying reparations.

It was also officially declared that I had assassinated the new heavenly emperor. There was a succession crisis in Yulong right now due to several people vying for the title, claiming they were the illegitimate children of the guy that died. One thing was for sure: Yulong was on its way out.

Ordinarily a nation would receive foreign aid or relief efforts after a crisis, but… Yulong didn't get anything like that. Nobody wanted to associate themselves with a nation of scoundrels and liars. To me, they were simply reaping what they sowed. I couldn't muster up a single damn.

I dropped the money into [Storage] and left the guild. I wondered how much money to give out to each soldier as a bonus. I decided that I'd be generous. They'd earned it, after all. As I mulled over the specifics, I walked over to the dungeon portals and checked in with the spy that Tsubaki had installed at the nearby market.

"Yo."

"Aha. Welcome, dear customer. I've a bargain for you today."

*Hm? Something happen?* As he spoke up, I began inspecting the goods.

"Several people have died recently."

"...Oh. Well, that sucks but... I guess it's a real risk when you go adventuring. Were they killed by magical beasts or something?"

"That's how it seems, at least. They simply didn't return... They were all low-ranked adventurers, so it stands to reason that they overestimated themselves and died as a result." *Probably got cocky and dug too deep. People are greedy. They should really prioritize their safety a little more, geez... It's smarter to pay attention to your own situation rather than put yourself at risk.*

"There is something a little strange about it, though. Their bodies have yet to be found. Only their guild cards have been recovered."

"Huh? I know that slimes melt down organic material, but what about their armor and stuff?"

"Ah, no... Well, perhaps you aren't familiar, but... there are those amongst the adventuring community who are... somewhat like hyenas." *What? There are people that loot their fellow man's corpse? I mean, it's a pretty scummy thing to do, but I guess it's not awful...*

It was considered common etiquette to hand items belonging to the deceased over to the guild. They'd then be able to pass those things on to the dead guy's next of kin. Still, it wasn't an enforced rule or anything. It was just a matter of good manners.

It reminded me of a story I'd heard from one of the guilds. Once there was a rookie adventurer who had used his enormous savings to buy himself an incredible set of armor. He was so pleased with it that he took every opportunity he could to brag to his peers about it. Several days later... the man's body was found in a dungeon. His expensive armor was nowhere to be found.

The situation was rather interesting. Was the armor stripped from his body after a monster killed him? Or was he murdered in cold blood by another adventurer who had set his sights on the man's treasure? No way to know.

Regardless, these dead adventurers were just regular rookies, so it was unlikely they'd been targeted and killed for any good reason.

"How many died?"

"We've found ten guild cards so far. Nothing else has been recovered, so we can't say for sure." *Geez... Ten people died?* My mood had soured a little. I decided it might be wise to create a safe zone on the top level that monsters couldn't access, or maybe some teleportation circles in the rookie areas so they could easily get back outside.

I said my goodbyes to the spy, and headed toward the portals.

I saw a group of youngsters heading toward the gate to Amaterasu. They were handing their copper over to the clerk. They looked to be around twelve or thirteen years old. In total they were a party of four. Two boys, two girls.

One of the boys was clad in scale mail, and he wielded a spear. The other young lad was wearing leather armor, and he had a bow on his back.

One of the girls looked like a novice mage. She was wearing robes and had a little magic rod. The other wielded an iron sword and wore leather armor much like the boy's. They looked like archetypal newbies going off to adventure.

The four of them passed through the Amaterasu portal and were off to the dungeon in a flash.

Now, in all honesty... I was a little worried about the kids due to the story I'd just been told.

*Should I follow them...? No, stalking's bad business... But I'd rather kids didn't go out there unprepared... Maybe I could set up an adventuring school or something... Yeah, that could work, I think. I could hire former adventurers to give kids survival tips. Still, how should I run it? I don't think we should charge a fee to enroll... Maybe they can pay back student debt after graduating? We could co-operate with the guild to track the quests and cards of students, or something...*

I decided to ask Relisha about it later on. She'd probably have better input.

"Hm, Touya?" I turned toward the voice to find Leen as the source. Paula was toddling after her. She was wearing her typical Gothic lolita outfit, and strolled along beneath the shade of her parasol.

"Oh, Leen. What brings you here?"

"I was just doing a little window shopping. Sniffing around for bargains, you know? And yourself?"

"Ah, well... I was thinking of making some modifications to the dungeon. I'm gonna install a safe zone that monsters can't enter, so people can get some rest."

"Heh... That sounds quite interesting. I'll tag along with you, then." Leen grabbed me by the arm without even asking.

*Hmph... You sure have been more aggressive in your approach lately... Are you that desperate to marry me?*

I was a little embarrassed since she looked around the same size as Yumina and a couple of the others... To a bystander, I probably looked like a doting elder brother.

We headed over to the toll booth. Leen took out a single copper coin from her pocket and handed it over to the worker. Her name was then written down on a small logbook.

Even if you weren't a member of the guild, you could still pay to pass through the gate. The only difference was that your name was manually recorded in the logbook. The guild card certainly made the process simpler, though.

I also paid a copper coin and put my name down. I didn't want to stand out too much by flashing my card around. I put down 'Takeda Shingen' as my name. There wasn't a rule against using a false name, after all. I decided that Takeda Shingen would be the fake name I'd use for stuff like this in the future.

We passed through the portal, and the dazzling sun bore down on us. Compared to the wintery Brunhild, the island was a tropical paradise.

I looked around uneasily, but I saw no sign of the rookies from before. I assumed they'd already gone into the dungeon.

Leen and I, along with Paula, strolled through the entrance. My faithful fairy friend put away her parasol and cast [**Light Orb**] in front of us.

"Shall we go down to the third floor?" If I recalled correctly, Amaterasu Dungeon had been scouted out to six floors at that point. I pulled up my map app and headed toward the first set of stairs.

"...Why, and how exactly, do you have this territory already mapped out on that contraption...?"

"...I'm just not going to answer. I really have nothing to say about it."

Leen muttered as she stared at the projected map. It wasn't like I expected the place to be fully mapped out for me or anything. It just wound up like that, really.

We made it to the stairs without any issue, then descended to the second level floor. We ran into the odd magical beast or monster, but I took care of them fairly easily. We eventually made it to the third floor, but it took us a decent while.

"I think I wanna make a rest area around here. It'll be a safe space where the adventurers can rest up a little bit. Just gotta find a suitable spot..." I brought up the map again to look for a good location. I'd also set the map to display any other adventurers who were in here, since I didn't want to get in their way. Plus, they might have ended up getting in my way, too.

"Isn't this spot fine? It's about midway between the stairs that lead up and down." Leen pointed at a fairly broad room with a few sprawling paths leading to and from it. It'd certainly make a good rest spot for any weary parties, and it was out-of-the-way enough to avoid if you wanted to. It seemed just fine to me.

We carried on to our destination, killing more beasts that came our way. The enemies were more annoying than anything else. Having an item like a 'repel' from those handheld games certainly would've come in handy.

We reached our destination and began looking around. I wanted to investigate the room for traps or hidden dangers before securing it properly.

I used [**Enchant**] and [**Program**] to monster-proof the room. Hostile creatures wouldn't be able to enter at all. Then, I began to inscribe letters on the wall. It was a fairly basic message, just detailing that magical beasts and monsters couldn't appear in the room, so it was a safe space to relax.

I decided to add my signature too, since I didn't want them thinking it was a trap.

"Signed by Mochizuki Touya... grand duke of Brunhild." I hoped it was enough to make them feel safe. Thinking about it reminded me that I hadn't seen those rookies anywhere. Then again, they were beginners, so they were probably just walking around the first floor.

I remembered their faces, so I decided I'd run a little search just in case. *Uhh... let's see... Display the regular adventurers with a blue icon, and display the particular newbies I'm thinking of with a green icon...*

*Huh... That's odd. They're on floor two already? And wait... there's more than four in the room. Huh, three more adventurers? Maybe they teamed up or something... Wait, something doesn't seem right here. What's with those movements? Are they in the middle of a battle with monsters or something?*

"There are seven, no? Why are they struggling so much?"

"Well, those four kids were totally amateurs. They felt like kids who had basically walked right out of a farm and picked up some weapons." I briefly considered that they might not be especially weak. After all, they could have just been up against a lot of enemies. Even Kobolds and Goblins could be deadly if you encountered more than ten of them at a time.

*Let's see... Highlight monsters and magical beasts... There we... Wait... There aren't any monsters in that room? Then... what the hell? It's not faulty, since I can see the indicators for monsters in other rooms... So, wait... No way...*

"...What does this mean?"

"...The other three adventurers... They're the ones attacking those kids."

There was trouble afoot.

We reached the second floor just in time to see the young boy with the spear being blasted into a wall. The archer and female mage were collapsed on the ground in a heap. Though the boy with the spear and the girl with the sword were clearly injured, they were still standing and defending their friends.

"Don't rough 'em up too much, retard. They're merchandise."

"Shut the fuck up, asshole. We're only in this situation because your deadbeat ass forgot the paralysis poison."

"Whatever, you two! Just do it quick, yeah? If any monsters show up it'll— Bauuggguuugh!!!" The obese man's commentary was cut short by a swift kick delivered to his face. My attack had sent him bouncing across the room like a rubber ball, where he landed in front of his comrades.

"Whuh— Who the hell are you?!"

"That's my line, asshole! Who are you guys?" One of them was fat, one of them was bald, and the other was lanky. They couldn't have looked like a more suspicious sort.

The tub of lard scrambled to his feet, wiping his nose. I was surprised that he'd absorbed the impact, honestly... Seemed like obesity had its perks.

"Good grief... Seems we made it just in time." Leen arrived alongside Paula. Immediately, lechery manifested on the faces of the three men. The lanky asshole started sauntering over toward me, weapon drawn.

Not long after, the other two started approaching as well. They probably saw Brunhild on my waist and assumed it was just a dagger. They were looking at Leen instead of me, though. Looked almost as if they were trying to appraise her worth.

"Mm... Sexy little thing, aren't you? Lucky us, eh boys? Hey, brat. If you care about your life, then shove off and leave the bitch here."

"...Huh?" Not long after, the other two started approaching as well.

"You deaf, kid? We said beat it. Leave the little girl behind, and me and my boys will have a bit of fun with her! Scram, idiot! You wanna die?!" I slowly walked over to the lanky moron, then let out a little sigh. Then, in a single swift motion, I brought my foot down upon his leg. *Crunch.* His bones splintered, and he was down for the count.

"GAUAUUUUUUGH!!!" The man screamed, clutching his smashed leg as he rolled around on the ground. His eyes welled up with tears, dribble and spit ran down his chin, and obviously his nose was a mess of snot. *Shut the hell up.* I kicked him in the side of the face.

"Ghuuuheeek!!!"

*You think I'd leave Leen with bastards like you? Don't delude yourself, dumbasses. Don't be so goddamn pathetic. I'll kill you.*

"Y-You piece of shit! Stop this at once!"

"We're Blue adventures, fuckboy! Think you can win against us?!"

"You talk tough, but you're not rough enough to throw down with the best of them. Vultures like you probably ranked up by stealing spoils from others, am I right? There's no way in hell a Blue adventurer would be as shitty as you. Don't you dare disrespect the name of the guild, you little bitch." I lashed out a kick, cracking one of the fat bastard's kneecaps. He collapsed under his own weight and fell on his face.

"Muggghuh... Mh-My lh-leg... Nnnghahhh!!!"

"E-Eek!" The baldy turned and ran, but it was futile. I pulled out Brunhild, aimed at his back, and pulled the trigger.

"Guh!" He took a paralysis bullet directly, then fell forward. *Some adventurer,* I thought. *What a coward. Blue rank? More like blue stank.*

"...That was more than a little extreme, Touya. You can color me several shades of surprised," Leen muttered quietly as she looked at the fallen men.

"Ah... Forgive me. I got mad when they said that stuff about you." It had been a while since I'd been that angry. The last time was when I was dealing with the idiotic prince from Lihnea. In all honesty, I had thought that my patience had gotten a little better, but it seemed I was still on far too short a fuse.

"Hmm... I'm a little bit happy you got so furious on my behalf..." Leen grinned a little bit at me.

*Ugh. That's embarrassing...* I turned away from Leen to hide my face. Then, I remembered the injured newbies.

"You guys good?"

"Y-Yes, we're okay... A little injured, but I'm fine... Klaus and Eon are in a worse state, though..." The boy with the spear motioned to his collapsed friends. They looked like they were just out cold, but I cast [**Cure Heal**] and [**Refresh**] on them all just to be on the safe side. The two on the ground then regained consciousness.

They wouldn't stop thanking me, but I did manage to get a few questions in edgewise. The three men had met up with the kids in the dungeon and promised them a safer hunting ground. Then, they just followed them. Pretty careless, really. But they were just kids.

They were brought off to this secluded area and attacked. The archer and the mage weren't frontline fighters, so they were knocked out of the battle faster due to the surprise nature of the attack.

"I guess these guys are kidnappers, then... People have been going missing, only bloodstains or guild cards left behind... It would be reasonable to assume they were eaten up by the wildlife here, but... now I'm starting to get a different idea."

"Y-Yeah! They said they were going to sell us to slave traders!" The sword-wielding girl raised her hand and spoke. I hadn't noticed her ponytail earlier. She was quite energetic.

*Still, slavers... That's no good.*

I walked over to the lanky man and thrust Brunhild's muzzle against his forehead.

"Answer yes or no. Nothing else. Are you the ones responsible for the missing adventurers lately?" The man nodded quickly. He was sweating bullets. It was as I'd expected.

Leen tilted her head to the side as she pondered.

"But... after kidnapping the adventurers, how did they transport them from the island? They wouldn't be able to use the portals..."

"That's pretty simple. They probably have a boat. Some kind of slaving vessel. Is that right?" The man nods just as quickly as he had before. I was right.

These islands were located due south of Sandora, after all. And, as far as I knew, the nation in which slavery was most prominent was none other than the Burning Kingdom of Sandora itself.

It was a country that used special collars to enslave people and turn them into living merchandise. It also meant that our missing persons were probably already lost.

"Are the missing adventurers already in Sandora?" He shook his head this time. I was surprised. It meant they hadn't shipped them all off... And *that* meant we could still save them.

The slaver ship was probably anchored somewhere nearby, but obscured. These assholes had clearly faked the deaths of several adventurers and stored them on the ship for processing later on.

I brought up my map and searched for boats in the area. Sure enough, there was a sizable boat moored off the coast of a smaller island to the north. I had found it.

With that, I had the whole case figured out. It also meant the three stooges here were of no more use to me. I subdued all three of them with [**Paralyze**] for the time being.

"Well, what now? I-If you want to inform the guild or the knights, I'll come with you..." The ponytail girl nervously spoke up. Her three companions were talking amongst each other. The situation was pretty dire, but I didn't think they quite understood. There was definitely some anxiety due to what had happened, but they seemed more excited than they should've been.

"Don't worry about that. I can handle it. Ah, that's right... We never introduced ourselves. This girl is Leen, and the little bear is Paula. I'm Mochizuki Touya. I'm the grand duke of Brunhild."

"Wh-Wh-What?!" All four of them stared at me in terror. Then, they crouched down on the floor and began bowing.

"Get up, geez. You don't need to do that kinda crap with me. I'm an adventurer at heart, you know...? I still go on quests even now." I pulled out my golden guild card as I spoke. Those kids had been tricked once already, so I at least wanted to provide some level of evidence.

"G-Gold..."

"Amazing..."

"Th-This guy has killed Dragons, Golems, and Demon Lords..."

"We gotta tell our dads about this..." Well, they definitely believed me. These kids were a little soft for this business, if you asked me. They'd end up getting hurt if they just believed everything they were told... Although they'd actually already ended up getting hurt because of that.

The four of them finally formally introduced themselves to me. Apparently they'd all come from Regulus, a village called Pyton to be exact.

The scale mail-clad boy with the spear was called Lop. The sword-wielding girl in leather armor was named Fran. The archer who wore similar leather armor was named Klaus. And finally, the mage girl was named Eon.

The impression I got was that Lop was loyal, Fran was bursting with energy, Eon was a total klutz, and Klaus was their leader. They were a bit of a ragtag party, all things considered.

"What are we gonna do? Help out the adventurers who got caught?"

"That's right. I found out where the slaver ship is, so I'm gonna go wipe them out."

"U-Uhm! Is there any way we could help you?"

"H-Hey now, Fran!" Fran suddenly spoke up, much to the chagrin of Klaus.

I was pleased that the kids had motivation, at the very least. I wasn't too sure that they'd be of much help, though. I definitely was in support of helping them gain a bit more experience, but at the same time... Well, I wasn't exactly sure what to do.

"Our enemy here are merchants that deal in human lives. They might even have slaves equipped for battle serving them. What I'm asking is if you're confident you can help here. In a worst-case scenario, you'll be enslaved yourselves."

"Ugh..." Fran looked down, seeming suddenly troubled. I wonder if she was feeling ashamed about her earlier loss.

They were older than Lu and Yumina, but younger than Elze and Linze. Even so, they weren't too far off my own age.

In the case of my party, we'd fought the Phrase, battled Dragons, involved ourselves in a coup, and so on. We had many rich experiences that allowed us to develop as a team... Even though those incidents were still my fault...

"Hmm... If they can't fight, can we not have them do recon?"

"Recon?" I quirked a brow at what she had said. *Decoys, huh...? Maybe...*

"Well, I said recon, but... I would recommend they infiltrate the ship and get themselves intentionally captured. If they pretend they got caught by these three and get aboard the ship, they'll be able to easily learn about what's going on with the other missing people."

"I guess so... But are these three dumbasses gonna obey?" I turned toward the three paralyzed men. It was true they might listen if I threatened them, but they probably didn't have good enough poker faces to go along with that level of deception.

"You dummy. Simply use [**Mirage**] and become part of the deception as well."

"Aha, smart thinking." *Yeah, that makes sense. If I disguise myself as one of those dumbasses, I can escort the rookies to the ship. That way we'll be able to infiltrate the place and get the captured people out safely. I don't want the adventurers being taken hostage, so this is probably a good idea, but still... Guess I could just use [**Invisible**] to sneak on to the ship myself and rescue them all a lot faster, though...*

I looked over to the four kids, but they were just staring at me with stars in their eyes.

*Guh... What's with these kids? They're not scared at all about maybe being made into a commodity? ...Man, fine. I won't trample over their resolve. Saying something like "You're dead weight, so beat it, kid" would just break their hearts at this point, and I'm not in the business of upsetting children. Hell, if I hurt them now, they might end up being discouraged from adventuring, so… I guess I'll pass on a little bit of the knowledge I've gained from my own quests…*

"…You kids wanna try it?"

"Yeah!!!" The kids cheered merrily. I wondered if it'd actually be okay… But I decided to go along regardless.

We all left the dungeon, and I warped the three kidnappers to Brunhild's jail. It'd cause too much of a fuss to carry them back through the portals. After all, if their allies were watching, they'd know the jig was up and escape.

I contacted Relisha and told her the basic gist of the situation. Those three would have their guild registrations erased, and their cards revoked. Even if they used fake names, they'd still be rejected. No more adventuring for those guys.

That was the guild's punishment for them, but I still had to decide how my country would handle them.

They'd been capturing newbie adventurers, taking all their stuff, and selling them into a life of servitude. It was a serious crime. If we went by Regulus law, then these guys would be getting the death penalty.

Unfortunate as it was in some people's minds, Brunhild didn't have the death penalty. Mainly because I hadn't created one. As I wondered about how to deal with them, I recalled something I'd read about in the Library.

Dark attribute magic was pretty much exclusively summoning, but apparently there used to be other applications of the element.

There was a spell that was the opposite of the Light element's recovery magic. It was a magic that sapped the life away from the target.

Well, actually killing them with it would take considerable effort and focus. The user would require incredible willpower, magical power, and skill with magic. I'd probably have been able to pull it off, but I wasn't especially motivated to try.

I wasn't saying I'd use this death magic on the kidnappers, by the way. There were other spells derived from that kind of spell.

These spells could be described simply enough. Effects included pestilence, fear, confusion, and life absorption.

In short, they were curses. Though maybe calling them curses was a little bit of a stretch.

The magic kind of worked like a promise. It was a system where if they broke the circumstances set by the caster, they'd become afflicted by the conditions. Curse magic that only triggered if the affected disobeyed. Kind of like "Cross my heart and hope to die, stick a needle in my eye." Except the needle actually goes in their eye if they mess up.

**"Brand, o Darkness. Sinful Brand: [Guilty Curse]!"** I invoked the curse and targeted the three imprisoned men.

The conditions were simple. "Do not knowingly commit crimes and hurt others." Each time they broke this curse with petty crime, they'd lose a finger to paralysis. Eventually it would spread to their arms, and then their legs. If they persisted, they'd lose all five senses. The final stage was paralysis of the heart, and that'd be a wrap. Of course, if they committed one large, heinous crime, it'd all trigger at once.

This magic worked similarly to enchanting. The effect would persist even if I died. It was an unbreakable curse.

I told the trio all the details of the brand they'd been marked with. Hurting others didn't only apply to physical abuse. If they hurt people on a deep emotional level, or tried to torment others, then it'd activate too. If they stole and the original owner was devastated, it'd trigger too, as would rejecting a woman's feelings if it ended up causing her to feel bad. I wasn't going to be lenient about just what caused the curse to go off.

I'd been kind enough to let them live, so it was a fair burden for them to shoulder. They needed to become ideal men to survive the punishment.

In all honesty, I didn't believe it was possible to live a life without hurting anyone. Maybe if they became hermits and lived away from civilization, but still... They'd only be surviving at that point, not living. Regardless, perhaps they appreciated that Brunhild didn't just have them killed like Regulus did.

As I told them about their punishment, the men gradually turned pale and fell to the ground. The brand of their curse appeared on their foreheads, marking them forever.

The fatass turned to the lanky guy and screamed.

"We're only like this because of you, idiot!" It made me wonder if he'd listened to a word I'd said. "Wuh?! Augh! M-My finger!!! I can't feel my finger!" The fatass started to cry as he prodded at one of his dead fingers.

*Isn't it obvious? You upset the lanky guy by screaming at him like that. It's simply your just desserts.*

Now that they'd seen the effects, I decided to banish them from Brunhild. *Where to send you... Oh, how about Yulong? The people there already talk shit about me, so you'll be right at home.*

I opened up a **[Gate]** to Yulong and shoved the guys through. *That's that. Case closed.*

*Oh. Wait. No. I still have to actually deal with the slavers, huh?*

I headed toward the forest on the island and waited for the cover of night. I felt a little bad for making the rookies wait so long, to be honest. Still, I couldn't have them wandering around. It'd look weird if one of the slavers saw them free, then captured only a bit later.

I'd left Leen with them, just in case they found themselves under attack by the local fauna.

After regrouping with them, I used a **[Gate]** to bring us all to the island with the slaver ship. All four of them were amazed. It was their first time, after all.

"Alright, then. Hand over your weapons. It'd be weird if captured victims still had their stuff." They handed their weapons over and I tossed them into **[Storage]** before pulling out a length of rope and tying them up. After that, I popped gags in their mouths. Naturally, they were bound in a way that was easy to escape from.

After that, I summoned a little mouse and hid it inside Lop's pocket. That way I'd be able to know more about the situation aboard the ship.

I used **[Mirage]** to add the finishing touches. I'd disguised myself as the baldy. One was too lanky, and the other way too fat, so cueball was closest to my own physique…

"Well?"

"You look identical… That's incredible…" Lop was amazed, evidently. I used **[Mirage]** once more to project a false image of the other two guys to my left and right.

The four of them prepared to be transported, and I made the illusory versions of fatty and lanky stand behind them, swords drawn. It'd look like they were being escorted, now.

"What about you, Leen?"

"I'm fine, thank you. I'll keep watch and ensure nobody escapes the vessel." Paula brought her hands up toward the sky. It was time to head to the slaver ship.

We found the ship. It was well positioned, shrouded in the shadow of a cliff.

There were two smaller boats making port on a nearby beach. Four men stood around a bonfire. They were grilling fish. Three of the four looked to be slaves.

They were pretty bulky, so they were probably combat-oriented slaves. The non-slave guy had a really bad overbite on the bottom row of his mouth. He kinda looked like a jerk. We left Leen and Paula in the cover of the trees, then moved toward them.

"Oh, good haul. I see you've been busy. Four at once! What a doozy." Overbite walked over to us and smiled a bit. He seemed impressed.

He walked around us and started looking the kids up and down.

"Two gold for the boys. Five for the girls. Seems fair to me."

"Deal. Hand over the cash."

"Huh? No hagglin' today…?"

"We're in a rush." I didn't want to talk too much and get exposed. Still, two gold and five gold respectively… That was like two hundred thousand and five hundred thousand yen… Buying out someone's life for cash like that was downright despicable.

They'd probably end up selling the people for a lot more to rich types in Sandora. Overbite handed the money over and let out a shrill, annoying laugh.

If I saw that guy again, I'd definitely be giving him a smack in the face.

I returned to Leen and canceled my spell. I hated looking like those bastards.

I used [Long Sense] to watch the four men. They finished eating their fish, put two kids into each boat, and started rowing toward the main ship.

"Infiltration complete."

"Indeed… I hope they get in touch with the other captured people soon, though. How many have gone missing, exactly?"

"Relisha said there were ten who were formally dead. Their guild cards were found, usually with blood nearby, so the guild assumed the worst. Uh… I think it was three men and seven women."

"Seems they're biased toward capturing girls, then."

"Probably because they're easier to grab, and they sell for more money. All of the captured adventurers were Black." From what I'd heard, newbie bullying wasn't uncommon in the guild. More experienced adventurers with shitty attitudes would use new recruits as bait for strong monsters. They even ended up taking most of their rewards as "tuition expenses" if they survived. In the end, the victims often wound up leaving the guild and going solo. It was despicable.

No matter the world, there were always those who looked down on newcomers. Those people often forgot that they too were new once as well.

Either way, I hoped all ten of the victims were safe. They were likely still alive. Hard to sell a corpse, after all. But that didn't mean they were safe. Their lives were hanging in the balance.

I synchronized my vision with the mouse in Lop's pocket. I saw the ship's deck, which meant they'd made it there safely enough.

My hearing was also synchronized. I heard voices around them. Sight and hearing was as far as I synchronized my senses, though. I tried taste once and immediately regretted it… I didn't want to know what a beetle tasted like, but the mouse had other ideas.

"Mr. Javert… I've brought four."

"Wonderful… They seem to be high quality stock. Young meat… Yes, they'll sell well." Overbite approached a plump man. He was rubbing his hands together as he looked at the kids. This guy was most likely the slave merchant.

He wore a fancy wool jacket, a silk sash with a golden dagger hanging from it, and some pointy shoes that bent upward at the end. He also had a long coat and what looked like a precariously balanced turban on top of his head. He looked like a fat, discount Sinbad the Sailor.

*Javert, huh…? I bet he's a slaver from Sandora. Probably a black market one, too.*

Even though Slavery was legal in Sandora, they prohibited kidnapping people and forcing them into servitude. Slavery was typically reserved for criminals, or those who willingly sold themselves into the service.

But that was only an official stance. There were many ways to become a slave in Sandora. Some forced others into debt, or tricked them into crime in order to make them slaves. Others simply kidnapped people and put them into market circulation.

Once you're a slave, your opinion isn't valid. Nobody would listen to you. Even if you made a fuss about being tricked or kidnapped, you'd be ignored.

The problem was the fact that Sandora's government never spoke about it. Their king and nobles all had slaves as well. They worked slaves until they expired, then simply replaced them with new ones. In Sandora, the life of a slave wasn't really seen as a life at all.

"Come on! Pick up the pace!" Overbite yanked at Lop's rope and dragged them all along.

All four of them were brought down to the lowest deck of the ship. There were two jails, divided by sex. There were three men and seven women there. The kidnapped adventurers. Lop's party was split up by sex as well.

After Overbite had left, the four of them turned to ask the names of their fellow captives.

The names matched those of the missing adventurers, so that was good.

They seemed weak due to lack of nutrition, but they hadn't been abused otherwise.

"Seems they're all fine... I can pull up a [Gate] right now and sort it out, then."

"You should let those children get some experience first."

"Hm... I guess a ship escape would be good for them."

"Quite. It's an important lesson in stealth and perception. Wouldn't you agree?" Leen smiled as she spoke. She was certainly right.

Lop's party began preparing their escape. I was prepared for this kind of situation, so I'd given them two particular items.

The first was a tiny knife that folded. It had a 5cm blade. Naturally, it wasn't a standard knife, either. It was forged of Phrasium, and could cut through anything at all. Escaping wouldn't be an issue at all so long as they used them wisely.

The second item was a measuring tape. It was about a meter long. I'd enchanted it with [Paralysis] so they could stretch it out and use it as a whip.

There were slaves built for battle aboard the ship. Those kids definitely couldn't win if they fought fairly. Plus, their enemies would mostly be fellow slaves anyway.

Lop's party cut their bindings apart and quietly escaped from their cells.

"Guess I better get going too, huh. I'll make it a little easier for the kids."

"Have fun, Touya." I deactivated the mouse's live feed and Leen saw me off as I exited the forest. I stood facing their ship, Brunhild in my hand. Then, I loaded the thing with [**Explosion**] bullets, though I took care to load the low-yield versions.

"Let's dance…" With a grin on my face, I aimed my gun at the ship's mast… and pulled the trigger.

The blast immediately made the thing collapse. It creaked and groaned, and then snapped under its own weight. Every man on deck started freaking out. Only natural, since part of their ship had just toppled into the sea.

"Wh-What happened?!"

"I-I don't know… There was an explosion of some kind!" Javert stormed out of the main cabin and demanded an explanation. It was at this point that I landed myself on the ship and revealed myself by the light of the moon.

"Wh— Who?!"

"I'm Mochizuki Touya. Touya's my given name. The brilliant grand duke of Brunhild at your service." Everyone on deck was completely speechless. The merchant didn't look as happy as he had before, his eyes filled with dread and confusion. He was completely and utterly flustered, which meant he was aware of his position.

"This island is Brunhild's territory. I've come to put an end to your illicit activity."

"I-Illicit?!"

"Don't take me for a fool, tubby. I know what you've been doing with the rookie adventurers from the nearby dungeons." He stood there, mortified. His jaw was slack. Sweat began to bead on his brow. He really didn't seem all that innocent.

"To be fair, we're a pretty small nation. I get it. We don't have a lot of laws established properly yet. But you know, we don't have many bad people in Brunhild. The worst we get is the occasional rough-housing traveler. Your actions have made me think a little bit harder about crime and punishment."

*If I hadn't come to the dungeon today, it wouldn't have just ended with Lop's party been taken away. There would've been countless more victims afterward... I have no idea how long it would've even taken me to realize what was happening.*

Punishment was the deterrent to crime, and I'd become lazy due to my personal lifestyle. I kept thinking about how things would be fine, so I closed my eyes to the cruelty of the world. Plus, I had Yumina and her Mystic Eye around, so I was mostly surrounded by legitimately good people.

Either way, crimes needed to be punished. And I needed to make that clear.

I had to draft a bunch of laws, and fast. I decided to reference Belfast's legal system before noting down my own later.

A lot of people had come to Brunhild after the dungeons were made, and they brought with them a litany of their own issues. Either way, what was important to think about at that moment was dealing with the slavers.

*Huh? I can see four little boats escaping the shift... Damn, Lop. You work fast. Guess there's no need to hold back now.*

"Hrmph. A grand duke has no business here! Deal with him!" Javert gave his order, and three burly slaves came running at me, curved swords at the ready.

"[Slip]." All three of them thudded onto the deck. Their swords ended up stuck in the wooden flooring.

They tried to stand, but found themselves falling down again. It seemed like my slipping spell had a slightly extended effect... I distinctly remembered it affecting a smaller area and not lasting as long when I'd first used it. I wondered if this was an effect of my own inner divinity growing.

"Wh-What are you fools doing?! Get rid of him!" Javert screamed, and the slaves all started clutching their heads in pain. He was using their collars to torture them.

I used Brunhild to fire a shot at the chubby jerk's feet. A weak explosive force threw the man off his feet.

"Whoa!!!" Chubby old Javert fell to the ground, blood dribbling from his nose.

"A-Augh! F-Forgive me! I-It was just uhm... m-my culture!"

"Then your culture normalizes abuse. If degrading people and turning them into slaves is your idea of the regular old thing to do, then do you really think you're worth forgiving?"

"H-Help me, you bastards..."

"Do you think the people you collared are going to rescue you?" I had no idea about this man or the life he'd been leading to this point, but I had no doubt in my mind that he was scum.

Speaking to him was pointless. I loaded some paralyzing bullets into Brunhild and shot them down at him.

He screamed out awkwardly, and then stopped moving.

I paralyzed the slipping slaves as well. They were probably being forced to co-operate, but they were still accomplices... It was some morally grey legal ground. I guess it would depend on whether or not they were enjoying it. It was a little more annoying to deal with than Javert. I didn't know if they'd been enslaved for criminal behavior, so I didn't know if it was okay or not to free them.

I also paralyzed all the remaining men on deck.

"Run search. Anyone remaining below deck."

"Searching... Search complete. Three individuals. All paralyzed and collapsed."

*Hm... Lop's party must have dealt with them. So that should be everyone. Twenty in total, eh... Half of them seemed to be slaves.*

*Wait, that reminds me... Where's Overbite?*

"Gah!" I heard a shriek from the shore. Then, I used [**Long Sense**] to check on the shore. Overbite was collapsed in a smoldering heap, and Leen was waving over at me. Seemed like he'd escaped at some point. Leen had it handled though, so I wasn't worried.

Lop's party had made landfall and were walking over to Leen. It was time for me to wrap things up.

I warped everyone from the ship over to the beach, just in time to see some of my own knight order making their way out from the forest.

I took Javert, his workers, and his slaves to the knights. Restrained, of course. We decided to lock them in the castle jail for the time being. I'd talk to Kousaka about them later on.

"All's well that ends well, eh?"

"Well, we'll still have to follow it up a bit." I casually replied to Leen as we walked along the beach. I looked back at the slaver ship, thinking to myself. *Should I confiscate it as Brunhild property...? Eh... The mast is broken.*

"U-Uhm, Your Majesty! The kidnapped adventurers are all good!" Lop came and reported in, but I pretty much saw the whole thing unfold through the eyes of the mouse anyway. I cast [**Refresh**] on the weary adventurers and took them all to the Silver Moon. There, I rented rooms for each of them. It was the least I could do.

I was planning on giving Lop's party about ten potions for their trouble. It'd be worthwhile for them to hold on to that stuff. Then, deciding that more detailed investigation would happen another day, I bid everyone involved farewell.

After that, I went over to the guild and informed Relisha of the finer details. I also asked her to return the guild cards of the people who were presumed to be dead.

"The guild regrets that this incident occurred. However, the guild is only a service mediator between clients and freelancers, so we cannot punish them. Other than revoking their memberships, there is little we can do… Officially, at least."

"Officially?"

"…Keep this just between us, but… in cases where we feel harm has been done to the image of our guild, we mobilize our Black Operatives. It's not necessary, however, in this case. You have meted out punishment enough."

*Black Ops, huh… What, like an assassination corps? That's kinda scary, to be honest… From what I understand, the guild exists all over the world. There are Guildmasters like Relisha that govern different regions, but there is actually one sole leader. I've heard they don't want to be in the public eye, though.*

I entrusted the guild with following up on the kidnapped adventurers. After that, I left with Leen.

It had gotten really late, so I took out my smartphone to look at the time. It was way past midnight…

I was getting really hungry, and I knew it would be unreasonable to ask Crea to make something when she was sleeping. I did have some grilled skewers in my [**Storage**]… and the guild's bar was right next door.

"Hey Leen, want me to treat you to some food?"

"Aha… I shall take you up on that venerable honor. I haven't eaten out in quite some time." I took Leen and Paula with me into the guild's bar. I put on a coat and hood just in case there were those that recognized me there.

It was a pretty big room, and I noticed a free table for four a little bit away, so we headed over there.

I ordered fried chicken and some fruit juice. No alcohol for me. Leen ordered a pasta, some salad, and a little glass of wine.

It wasn't long before the waitress brought our food over, and we began greedily chowing down. The food was great. I'd eaten at the Silver Moon a few times, but dining out at a bar seemed quite fun as well.

All the adventurers were laughing, cheering, and making merry.

It seemed like the bar had gained a lot more patrons since the dungeons were opened. It was hard to dislike the atmosphere here, even if the occasional drunkard ruined the fun.

We left the bar after our meal. I checked again, and it was still extremely late... Or, early. Matter of perspective. Most of the shops had closed down. There wasn't any kind of entertainment district in Brunhild's castle town, either. My country had nice, peaceful evenings.

Old man Naito relayed propositions from merchants and contractors to build casinos and brothels, but I left those executive decisions to him. I personally didn't see the need to have such gaudy venues. If they ended up coming in and causing trouble for my people, I'd close them down.

I needed to keep a watchful eye out, too. I didn't want any shady businesses setting up shop. It'd be beyond a joke if Brunhild became a breeding ground for trouble under my nose.

I remember hearing that some slaves were forced to work in brothels over in Sandora, too... I didn't want any of that going on here.

"Is it a pointless dream to wish slavery could be abolished?"

"I'm pretty sure it'd go if you smashed the hell out of Sandora. Pfftahaha…"

"N-No, that's not really what I meant…" I glanced over at Leen with curious eyes. Her cheeks were flushed… She almost looked drunk.

I heard that slavery was gradually being phased out around the world through social change anyway. Yulong had been a great advocate of slavery, so even if Sandora remained, it was nice that at least one of them was gone.

Yulong didn't use the obedience collars, though. They just drew up contracts and enforced indentured servitude. They didn't treat slaves nearly as badly as the people of Sandora did. Which was funny, given the country was awful in every other aspect.

"Sandora was founded by the chief of a desert tribe built by slaves. They used slavery to build a great force and wipe out or assimilate the other tribes in the area. The first king of Sandora was known as the Slave King." *The Slave King, huh…? Doesn't that name kind of give off the vibe of him being a slave himself? Maybe he actually was one to begin with. Still, if that was the case, he could've done something nice and abolished slavery after founding the nation…*

I mused that abolishing slavery in a place like Sandora would be pretty rough if it was so deeply ingrained in their society.

Leen wanted to feel the evening breeze on her skin, so we strolled home together. She was definitely drunk. She casually swayed side to side and then clung to my arm. Her cheeks were dyed red, and so were mine… but not because of booze. I attempted to compose myself and walked down the road with her.

There were four knights guarding the castle, but they stood down once they saw us. They were wary at first, but once we came into the light they seemed happy and waved us off.

After nodding to the guards, we entered the castle. Suddenly, we came face to face with Ripple. She was an artifact creature that operated as our very own security camera. When she saw me with Leen on my arm, she jumped right out of her painting and started screaming.

《Danger! Danger! Master, you're in danger! You need to be careful, it's almost too late! Hurry, prepare yourself f— Oh no… I wasn't fast enough…》

"Wh-What the heck?!" Ripple smiled wryly and then vanished on the spot. I had no idea what she was trying to warn me about, but it almost felt like she whispered "Good luck" before fading away. *What the hell was that?*

"Welcome home, Touya… You're rather late."

"Ah, Yumina… I'm… home…" My voice became quieter as I looked up and realized what I was faced with.

Yumina, Lu, Elze, Linze, Yae, and Hilde were all standing there, gazing at us. If Sue had been there, it would've been a full gathering of fiancees.

They were smiling, but their eyes projected danger. I felt anger emanating from their forms for some reason.

"U-Uh… Is something wrong?"

"We've a teeny tiny matter to discuss… This way. You too, Leen."

"Huh? Uh… Sure." Leen casually answered, but I didn't think she understood the threat. Yae and Hilde descended the stairs and grabbed me from either side.

*Wh-What the hell…? You don't need to forcibly escort me!*

"Right this way, Touya. This is the right course of action."

"Good grief, Touya-dono… Resign yourself to fate. It is far easier this way, it is."

"No, nooo! I didn't do anything wrong!!!" I internally and externally screamed for mercy as my mind filled with nothing but question marks. They dragged me away and completely ignored my pleas.

*What the hell did I do now?!*

"Don't think we haven't noticed things have changed between you two recently." The girls sat at the table, and Yumina began to talk. Leen was seated with my fiancees, but I was made to sit on the floor. *This is a little cruel, isn't it...? But I guess I'm kinda used to it at this point... Haaah...* It seemed that being forced to the ground by these girls was becoming a more common occurrence. "Leen. You love Touya, isn't that right?"

"...I can safely say that I do. My passion isn't quite on your level, but he is a man that I find suitable to my needs. I would be happy to be married to him until one or both of us die."

"I see... Well—"

"I'm not interested in him for Babylon's legacy, or his status as Grand Duke of Brunhild. I simply like him for who he is. He's charming, and kind. That's all there is to it." Leen interjected as Yumina spoke up again, clarifying her intentions. After she finished speaking, she stared Yumina in the eyes.

After a while, Yumina's expression became a little more gentle, and she smiled.

"Very well, then. You have my approval, Leen. I think you'd make a wonderful bride for Touya. What do you all think?" Yumina looked to my other fiancees. Yae raised her hand.

"I do not have any problems with this, I do not."

"I-I don't have a problem either..." Muttered Linze.

"Nope, no real problem here." Grinned Elze. The two sisters raised their hands as they spoke. Seeing their actions, the other two quickly put their hands up as well.

"I cannot say I object, either."

"N-No, me neither!" Hilde and Lu hadn't spoken with Leen much. But they still had a good enough grasp on her personality to read her as a person, scant as their interaction was.

Leen had been involved with me for longer than they were anyway... But even I couldn't have seen the situation developing like this. I was dumbstruck.

"I also don't believe Sue would oppose this if she were here, either. Speaking on her behalf as her cousin, I'd like to welcome you into the fold. Congratulations, Leen."

"Wonderful. Thank you so much." Yumina and Leen smiled at each other and gently shook hands. There wasn't even any room for me to comment at this point. I didn't have any personal reason to oppose what had been decided, but still... Well, Leen was mature, dependable, and very cute, so I figured it'd be alright.

If Yumina was the de-facto leader of the fiancees, then Leen would definitely fit in as the vice-commander.

Still, that brought the number of brides to eight. That meant I was one step away from completing the set. I couldn't help but wonder if the situation would've gotten this far if that damned doctor had just kept her future-telling to herself.

It kinda felt like Yumina and the others were eager to accept girls until the total came to nine... They probably couldn't relax until all nine were found. Still, they didn't accept Pam, so they were at least putting some thought behind it.

"Leen is now a sister in arms, she's one of Touya's fiancees, and our kindred spirit."

"H-Huh…? A-Aha… Y-Yes, I suppose I am."

"Now… Just where were the two of you this evening?"

"Eek!" A funny noise came from Leen's mouth. The other five surrounded her, emanating a silent pressure from their smiles.

"W-W-Wait just a moment! L-Ladies, you're misunderstanding, I promise!"

"Out until the early hours of the morning… Just the two of you… What else could it have possibly been, what else?" Paula flailed her arms in response to Yae's interrogation, as if to say "Hey! I was there too y'know!" But she was completely ignored. The twins came around the fairy's sides, staring daggers into her.

"I-Is it possible that…"

"Y-You two did… *it*?!"

"What?!" Both Leen and I yelled out in unison. *Do you mean THAT?! Wh-What the hell?!* Leen went red as a beet. So did Elze and Linze.

"Wh-Wh-Wh-What are you even saying?! O-O-Of course nothing like that went on!" Leen went into a panic while her face got even redder.

*Hah… That's a pretty cute reaction… It's a response more fitting the size of your body than the number of your age, though.*

The encroaching girls, upon seeing Leen's freak-out, eased up a bit.

Leen was in a state of panic and couldn't speak, so I explained the events of the evening in her stead.

"Well, that's understandable… But you should have sent a message to the castle if you were going to be this late."

"Ah… I-I'm sorry."

149

"Plus little Kohaku and the others let you relay mental messages, don't they?"

"Oh. Right." It had completely slipped my mind. I'd been running all over the place without making use of that at all. I didn't send a single message home to the castle, so the girls were probably worried sick or wondering where I was.

I had blindly believed there was no reason to worry, but that had been a little bit of selfishness on my part.

I didn't want to upset the people precious to me. Quite the opposite, in fact. I decided to be more mindful going forwards.

"We wouldn't know what to do if you went and left us behind, idiot."

"That is correct, it is. Let us know if you are doing something dangerous, yes?"

"You already wrecked that empty house, remember?" Elze, Yae, and Linze let out quiet sighs. *You're seriously still going on about that?! I-I just thought I could control a fireball like a missile... It's not my fault!*

I wondered if this was how a drunk man felt after returning home to be yelled at by his wife. I felt pretty whipped, regardless. I definitely didn't want to be a domineering husband, I respected the independence of the girls. But still, I was clearly upsetting Yumina and the others. They were all on good terms with each other, too. I hadn't heard of a single squabble between them. That made me the problem.

"At any rate, just contact us if you're staying out late, alright? We're not going to keep you on a leash, just keep us informed! Alright?"

"Y-Yeah, I got it..." Each one of them berated me more after that, until I finally got to go to my bed as the sun rose. They made me promise a lot of things, but the whole thing just felt like an unjust punishment.

Individually they were all sweet and soft, and I felt calm when I stood by their side… But when they ganged up on me I was utterly defenseless. I wasn't given any room to speak at all. It seemed like it was one of those things I just had to shut up and accept.

*Man, I'm beat… Zzz…*

After I woke up, I headed over to Kousaka and told him what had happened the day before. He immediately set to work on a rough draft of laws based on the ones in Belfast. The more specific ones would require my approval, though… I decided to save that for later…

This world was socially on the same level as the Edo period: they had death penalties and exiles in place. Other countries used forced labor like mining, but there were no mines in Brunhild.

Apparently most countries used capital punishment because of troubles caused in the nations that abolished it. If you simply banished a violent criminal, there was a chance they could cause trouble in another country. That being said, I didn't think just killing people was an ideal way to go about it.

Those slave collars were powerful artifacts used to punish criminals, and I approved, but only if they were put on people who had committed serious crimes. I wondered if I could modify one.

If we synced our laws up with Belfast's, Javert would definitely be killed. That honestly seemed fair, given his litany of foul deeds. I couldn't just give him a slap on the wrist, he'd been trafficking humans.

The main issue was what to do with the slaves and sailors on his ship. I figured I'd have Yumina use her Mystic Eye to check over the slaves at least. I'd free the good-hearted ones.

I headed towards the Silver Moon while thinking that over. I was a little worried about the adventurers that I had helped free the day before. Didn't want them suffering from trauma or anything due to their ill treatment.

I went in and spoke to them, and fortunately they had all resolved to continue adventuring. I told them to be more wary in the future. There was no need to rush, after all. It was better to slowly become stronger.

I told them to head over to the guild to get their cards back. Part of me felt a little guilty, but I was just glad they were safe.

I slept in till noon so I decided to have my breakfast/lunch at the Silver Moon. Lop's group ended up joining me for the meal.

They seemed apprehensive at first, but quickly settled in once I ordered five full lunches from Micah.

"Hm... There's a dungeon near your home village, then?"

"It's nothing like the island dungeons, but yeah. It's more like a cavern. There's a ruin inside it, though... We used to play in there when we were little kids." That sounded a little dangerous to me, there could've been dangerous wildlife in that cave!

"We'd found Giant Bats and wolves now and then, but the four of us managed to take care of them. I think those victories helped make us a little overconfident... But we've learned a little more humility after exploring a real dungeon." Fran spoke up, more of a mutter than anything. Wolves were certainly a far cry from Goblins and Kobolds. Intelligent monsters that used weapons were different from mindless beasts, after all. Still, that meant Lop's party had joined the blue-rank idiots despite their fear. I was sure they'd become promising adventurers.

"Well, just don't overdo it. Learn from your mistakes. Also, don't let people sucker you in with sweet words. There'll more often than not be an ulterior motive there. Every rose has thorns, and nothing in this world comes for free." The four of them nodded slowly. It seemed like they'd taken the lesson to heart. Really the fact that other adventurers had come and told them about a good hunting spot should've been a red flag. There'd have been no benefit to potentially decreasing their own gains by inviting newbies over. A certain amount of doubt was surely healthy, but at the same time it was important to trust others a little.

"Uh-Uhm, Your Highness... Can I ask something about this little guy...?"

"Hm?" Eon, the party's mage, showed the little white mouse that I'd summoned. I had completely forgotten about him.

To be honest, I was still worried about them. It's why I decided to leave the mouse with them. He was a summoned magical beast known as a Snowmouse. I had heard they were quite powerful in groups, but I wouldn't have believed that by looking at one alone.

I didn't know if this world had basic household mice, actually.

The Snowmouse had a magical passive effect known as Enhanced Senses. It allowed the person nearest to him to sense danger, preventing ambushes and other incoming disasters.

"I'll let you guys take care of him. He's pretty smart, and he can tell when there's trouble around. Also he has a mental link with me, so you can talk to him and send messages to me in an emergency." Eon smiled and nodded as I spoke. It seemed like she'd taken a liking to the little guy. I was pleased to see they were getting along. That being said, I didn't want a bunch of dumb messages being beamed into my head daily.

We finished up the meal and parted ways. The Snowmouse, now perched on Eon's head, waved at me. *Huh... I guess he really is smart.*

Something in the lunchtime conversation had piqued my attention. The cave that the four of them had mentioned... The ruins they mentioned made me think that it could be related to Babylon.

They were from Pyton Village in Regulus, if I recalled correctly. I searched on the map and it wasn't all that far from Brunhild. I was surprised that it was so close. The scout birds I'd sent out had probably missed it.

Or perhaps they just weren't able to see into the cave because they were high in the sky... No, that couldn't have been it. I had heard that birds were about the same as humans at night, vision-wise. They just didn't act at night because food was more scarce. There were still nocturnal birds like owls, though.

It was more likely that they'd just overlooked it. I'd find out for sure once I actually got there.

I invoked [Fly] and sent a message to Kohaku to inform the girls I was off investigating. They'd all gotten upset just the night before, after all. I didn't want to be lectured for two days in a row...

*Well then, guess I better check it out!*

Pyton village was in the southwest of Regulus. It was a pretty plain and quiet village nestled in some mountains near the Belfast border. It gave off the image of a peaceful quiet little mountain town.

I didn't want to cause a fuss or alert the villagers, so I landed in a nearby forest and pulled up my phone to look for the cave. I found it fairly close by.

"Huh, it really was near. I guess that makes sense, though... Those kids did play here." The cave was just a little ways up a rocky area near the town. Wasn't very big, either. The entrance was narrow, only one person could go through at a time. It seemed more like a thin tunnel than a cave, but once I got inside it opened up a bit.

It would probably be more apt to call the cave an entrance to the inner ruins. There were probably other entrances once, they must've just been covered by various means over the years.

A Giant Bat attacked me after I walked a little further in. Naturally it died in seconds. *Hm... The kids beat these things up? Guess they really are weak... Doesn't look like it'd be able to do much damage.*

After a while, I found an obsidian cube.

One side was around seven meters tall and wide. It was cold to the touch, as well. There was no doubt in my mind. This was a Babylon ruin.

"Alright, then... There's gotta be a way to get inside this thing." I inspected the cube thoroughly. I couldn't find anything like a switch that might open it up, though. There wasn't any groove on it like that other time, either. I wondered what the secret was. I mused that perhaps there was a wall that would let me pass through if I touched it... But alas, no luck.

"Hmph... What's with this thing...?" I considered using [**Modeling**] to force a hole open... But I couldn't shake the feeling that it would end poorly. This was something I needed to do on my own. But, no matter what... I couldn't find anything resembling a way inside.

I prodded here and there, but I was rapidly running out of ideas.

"Oh, come on... I've tried everything. Every side, even the top! What else is... Oh." *No way... Beneath, maybe?* I dug a trench using earth magic, careful not to let the cube fall or move. Then I jumped down and inspected it from below.

*Gotcha.* The bottom of the cube had a small dot indent in it, kind of like a 'one' side on a die.

"This should be it, then…" I touched the dot with my hand, and I found myself being pulled into the cube.

I looked around and found the regular spellstone pillars. It was dark, but the familiar shine of each stone was there in the black.

There was something unusual, though. The teleportation circle was on one of the walls, rather than the floor. The six pillars were also jutting out sideways from one of the walls.

"Waiiit a second… Shouldn't that be the floor, then? That means I entered from the side…" I figured they'd made some kind of mistake when the cube was placed in the cave. It was stupid to have the entrance be below to begin with; it honestly seemed like an error. When I thought about a six-sided die, I remembered that if the 'one' side was below, then the 'two' side would be on the side. They must've mistakenly placed the wrong side down, which meant I had to crawl under and through the single dot.

"Ugh, come on… Don't make dumb mistakes!" I used [Fly] to keep myself on the circle and then poured my magical power into the pillars. After that I stood sideways, feet planted firmly on the side of the wall. It felt weird as hell. *I'm not a ninja! This doesn't suit me… N-Ninja Arts… Wall-Stand Jutsu! Pffft…*

I added the final touch by pouring Null magic into the circle. It lit up in a flash, and just like that I was teleported away.

"Welcome to the Babylon's s— raughuhgh!"

"Huh?!" The light began to fade when I suddenly felt a dull pain in my stomach. I'd been headbutted. *Gah?! An ambush?!* From what I could discern, the terminal gynoid had recklessly ran over towards me, tripped, and smacked her head into my belly.

"Awawa! Forgive-a me! I was so excited to-a finally meet you that I went and slammed-a right into your side!"

"Fine, fine! Just get off me already!" The girl had knocked us both to the ground and she wouldn't stop muttering. It was pretty embarrassing because she was still on top of me. The girl had... assets. Not quite as impressive as Flora's, but impressive all the same. It was awkward.

"I'll get-a right up. Whoa, whoa!"

"The hell are you doing...?" The girl stood up and immediately began wobbling all over the place. And then she did it. She stumbled and, with all the weight of her body, brought her foot down on my crotch. "HNNNGH!" *Nhhh.... Mhhh.... Khhh....?! Hhh...!* I fainted. There was nothing else I could even do. It was the single most powerful attack I'd ever received in this world and the last. It hurt more than a direct hit from a Phrase. *Oh-Oh God... W-Will recovery magic work...?! Nngh... Gh...* [R-Rhh... Refresh]*...! Gah! I c-can't focus! My jewels... My jewels!*

"Mamma mia. Are-a you okay?"

"Ngh... Nnnhho..." I grit my teeth together and bashed my fists against the floor. It hurt. I was breathing heavily, I was sweating profusely. *I'm... Done... It's... t-too much...*

Eventually the pain subsided and I staggered to my feet. Then the girl looked at me and saluted. She was shorter than Cesca, or at least I thought so at a glance. She smiled and opened her mouth.

"Let-a me introduce myself! Welcome to the Storehouse of Babylon! My-a name is Lileleparshe! Just call-a me Parshe for short."

**"IT'S YOUUUUUU?!"**

"Eeeeeek?!" *I've finally found the madwoman! She's the one who let that immortal jewel thing fall down and ruin the Takeda house in*

*Eashen! She's the one responsible for the Blockbracer and Drainbracer helping that guy who started the coup in Regulus!*

I'd heard about her clumsiness from the other Babylon sisters, but now it was my precious jewels that had learned the truth first-hand. "Sit your ass down little lady! You need a stern talking to!"

"Wh-What! Why is-a this happening-a to me?!" I wondered if she was even aware of the trouble she'd caused. I decided to explain exactly what she'd done.

I told her about the suffering of the people on the surface as a result of the artifacts she'd carelessly let drop. Then I told her about all the troubles she'd gotten me into as a result.

"Are you sorry?!"

"Aah… I-I'm-a sorry… I wasn't aware of-a the troubles I'd caused!" Parshe let her shoulders sag. She knelt on the ground with sad eyes, and her ponytail trembled slowly. Maybe I had gone too far.

"Just… Take more care going forwards, alright? All the other gynoids were concerned about the Storehouse."

"Hmm? You've-a met other Babylon terminals?"

"With the exception of the Research Lab, I've met them all. Let me introduce myself, I'm Mochizuki Touya. The other Babylons have accepted me as their master."

"Wowee... Then I guess I'll do-a the same. Roger that... Airframe-a Number Twenty-Six, Lileleparshe, presents herself to you! Treat-a me well, Master." Parshe stood up and smiled once more, flashing a salute. That sure was a quick one-eighty. I wondered if she'd really reflected on her mistakes. Parshe quickly moved up towards me, almost making a lunge for my face. *Uh oh. I know that move...*

It was the eighth time at this point, and I no longer had the will to resist. It was inevitable, so I took it. I gave up on resisting, so I stood there and waited for it. Then Parshe stomped on my toe.

"Ow-mmmf!" Her tongue slipped past my lips and began swirling around in my mouth. But that's not what I was moaning about. It was my foot! She was crushing my foot! This girl was standing on her tip-toes to kiss me and she was crushing my goddamn foot! My big toe felt like it was gonna crumble! *Why the hell are you this clumsy! Is this even clumsiness?! You're a walking disaster!* "That's-a complete registration! Your genetic information has-a been stored in my banks, Master. The Storehouse now-a officially belongs to you... So why-a do you look so uncomfortable?" Parshe tilted her head to the side in confusion. *What the hell do you mean why! You just stomped the hell out of my toe!* I sat on the ground clutching my poor foot. I considered invoking [**Shield**] around her as a precaution.

"Well, regardless of-a that... Let-a me show you around. Onwards!" Parshe skipped off without a care in the world. Then she fell flat on her face. I figured this was just normal for her.

I saw a large dome-shaped building as I came out from the undergrowth. Well, it wasn't extremely large. It was about the size of an above-average house. It also looked just like an igloo, one of those Inuit homes made from snow. At least that was the closest approximation I could make.

I passed through the gates and came to a pure white room full of equally white cubes. They were about fifty centimeters tall, and they were that long as well. There was one black monolith in the middle of the room, too.

"You know... I kind of imagined there being... Stuff here. It's a storehouse, isn't it?"

"The artifacts, personal funds, raw materials, public and private records, and other such matters are-a stored in the basement. At one-a point we had a minor breach in an outer wall, but it was-a quickly repaired." *That's probably when the jewel and the other stuff fell out... At least it's patched up now.*

"You can use-a this machine to call up items. Look here..." Parshe put her hand on the monolith and it began to whir. One of the cubes on the ground in the distance fell through the floor, and a similar cube rose from the floor in front of me.

I looked closer and found small lettering on the surface of the cube. It seemed to be written in ancient Parthenese. It looked like every cube had a unique identifier.

Parshe touched the cube and it opened up like a treasure chest. To my amazement, it was filled with golden coins.

"The boxes can't-a be opened by anyone but you or myself. Even Doctor Babylon wouldn't-a be able to do it." *Huh, I see... So I effectively have the keys to the treasury. So then... All of this is mine? That's great. I'll use it well.*

I took out one of the golden coins from the box. It had a shape I didn't recognize. But then I remembered seeing something similar when I'd first met Ende. That must've meant these were coins from Partheno.

That made sense, in all honesty. The Storehouse was five-thousand years old, after all.

But that made the money worthless to me. I thought about smelting it all and selling the raw product. Taking it to an antique dealer was out of the question. They wouldn't believe something from so long ago would be in such incredible condition. It'd just get written off as fake.

"Ohh, right! Are there any Frame Gear blueprints in here?"

"Oh, the Frame-a Gears... Yep. We have-a those..." Parshe touched the monolith again and the box of coins sank into the floor. Another box quickly rose in its place. They looked identical. Without the serial codes I wouldn't be able to distinguish them at all.

I did what Parshe did earlier and touched the box. It creaked open. I stared at the contents, horrified. I closed the box.

"...Parshe... Send it back... You made a mistake. Now. Send it back. Now. Please."

"Huh? Ah, that's-a my bad... I got the number wrong." Parshe touched the monolith once more and the box sank into the floor. I turned away from her. My face was beet red and I was sweating bullets.

If you want to know what was in the box... It was just toys... Just... Adult... toys... I quietly reaffirmed my hatred for Doctor Babylon. I... didn't even know they made ones like that...

I opened up the new box and found a bunch of weird cylindrical containers. I tried popping one open to see what was inside.

What I found definitely resembled a blueprint. There were lots of different pictures and fine details and annotations.

I couldn't read it. The solution was to use translation magic, of course. But I still couldn't read it... It was way too complex to understand. Either way, this was a victory. We could finally create stronger Frame Gears. We couldn't modify the Frame Gears we already had, but now we'd be able to make them from scratch. In short, we could make custom Frame Gears.

*Heheh... Should I make one with a tank as its lower half? I wonder if I can... I should search online for different robot designs... I can't think of much other than heavy armor units, mobile suits, and backline support ones right now... Hehehe... I'm getting excited?! I can't help it! I'm a guy, it's too cool!*

"So, can you do it?"

"Yessir I can. I might be able to make Ether Liquid unnecessary, sir! Or, uh... Rather... I can probably make it so we don't need to change the Ether Liquid ever again, sir!" We were in the workshop. Rosetta was explaining certain blueprints we'd found in the Storehouse.

Ether Liquid amplified the magical power of a Frame Gear's pilot and spread it throughout the mech. Up until now we'd been using it as a raw fuel, but the cores of the new models took magic from sunlight and the surrounding atmosphere. It was kind of like transitioning from cells to solar panels.

But we needed crystalline material from dead Phrase to make the new power devices. It seemed like Doctor Babylon had noticed the unique qualities of the Phrase and figured out how to harness them for our benefit.

Either way, it allowed Ether Liquid to circulate through the machine without losing any of its magic. We wouldn't have to change out the fuel anymore.

"Well, sir! This new system is a conceptual one! We can assemble various parts and put them on Bone Frames. It should allow us to assemble unique varieties of Frame Gear, sir! In other words, sir! The new way of making Frame Gears has no predetermined form!"

"So we can build them as we want…? Or uh… It's more like if we can't figure out what we want, we won't be able to make it?"

"That is correct, sir. We could hypothetically slap anything we want together, sir! But it'd just create an ill-functioning hunk of scrap!" I didn't want us to waste our resources like that. But at the same time, I was eager to start experimenting with what we could put together.

"We must consider strength, armor, magical output, precision, mobility, and equipped weaponry, sir! This may be obvious, but if we make it heavily armored, it will have impaired speed! If we increase the output, it'll drain magic faster! If we consider your positively ridicu— Er, incredible mana reserves, sir, then we may be able to make whatever the hell we want! But that won't work for everyone, sir!" *Well sorry for having a ridiculous magic pool… But geez, what do I do? I have a lot of magic, yeah… But it'd be best to make Frame Gears that others can use. I should probably think about making specialized Frame Gears that fit specific people. Elze's should have a focus on power and speed, for example!*

Still, the specialized Frame Gears wouldn't be usable by anyone but the person they were designed for. Plus there was the fact that gradually using a Frame Gear made it accustomed to you and vice-versa, so they'd really just be personal units in the end.

"First thing's first, sir! We'll call the Mini-bots to the Storehouse! Monica and myself are insufficient for this task, sir." That was fair. I noticed two of the helper robots wandering around the workshop. They were incredibly skilled, despite their weird looks. They lacked the ability to think for themselves and could only obey rigid commands, but their versatility was nothing to scoff at.

I temporarily halted production of the Chevaliers so the workshop would be able to start building these new Frames. We'd made a lot of Chevaliers over the last few months, so I didn't mind putting it on pause for a little while.

"Alright, then… Let's try making a Frame Gear for Elze. I want you to prioritize speed and power. Make the limbs heavily armored, too. Don't worry too much about conserving magical power. We can always tweak that later."

"Sir yes sir!" I decided to start with Elze's Frame Gear because her fighting style was the simplest. Punching and kicking the enemy until they were down. It was a tried and tested method. It wouldn't need to be balanced or tweaked too much thanks to that. It was basically a model specialized for a single purpose.

I left Rosetta to it and headed to the Storehouse.

"Oh, Master. It's-a you." I entered the building and found Parshe there. She was wearing traditional shrine maiden's clothing, a red hakama over a white robe. I had never seen a shrine maiden who had her hair in a ponytail before, though… Well, it wasn't fair to apply the logic of my old world to this one anyway.

I had forgotten about all the stuff I'd passed over to Zanac, so I was surprised to see her in such a culturally familiar garb. It was an odd choice… Having someone this clumsy as a shrine maiden was a little much… I wasn't entirely sure that God would be okay with it.

"I've-a cataloged everything in the Storehouse for you. There are-a one-thousand-and-ninety-three items in total, Master."

"Wow, that's a lot." I flipped through the list she'd given me. There were things in there that I recognized, and some things that I didn't. There was also stuff on the list I knew I'd never want to look at. I decided that we didn't need the "Ultimate War Panties," the "Deadly Swimsuit," or the "Bikini Armor," for example. It would be better to separate them off entirely. Some things were better left sealed away.

*What's this...? "Breast Enlarging Medicine"...? Better not let anyone ever find out about this... This could destroy nations.*

"Parshe. Don't show anyone else this list, got it? And don't tell anyone about things available in the Storehouse unless you have my express permission. Got it?"

"Got it!"

Breasts... Big... Little... Everyone has them. Bigger, smaller, we needn't worry about such things. Bread is delicious. Rice is delicious, too. Neither invalidates the other! That being said, some people did prefer rice over bread... The other way too. I personally enjoyed both. I was a little saddened, though. Because I knew too many men in this world had eyes only for those big, round things.

Either way, I was getting off-topic.

"That reminds me. There should be Ether Liquid in storage here. Have it delivered to Rosetta at the workshop, and Monica at the hangar."

"Roger!" Parshe touched the monolith and nine cubes came out of the floor. I checked over them and, sure enough, they were all five-hundred milliliter bottles of the familiar fluid. It really did look like soda...

The mini-bots lifted them up over their heads and left the Storehouse.

"Parshe, what're these items with slashes through their names?"

"Ah! These are items that-a we've lost…" She muttered in quiet disappointment. I saw the Blockbracer and Drainbracer on the list, but I didn't see the immortality jewel on there at all…

*Oh, is it maybe this one…? The Eye of the Grave… I guess the guy who found it didn't know its actual name.*

"Then that means Lestia's Holy Sword is this Recovery Blade… And Ripple is the Living Frame. Neat." Even excluding the items I'd seen, there were a few unaccounted for artifacts. Searching for them would be a pain in the ass. Plus it wasn't likely that the people who had them would just give them up if I asked…

As far as I knew, there was no way for me to find them. Even if I knew what they were called, it wasn't like my search magic could find stuff I wouldn't recognize at a glance. It was unfortunate, but the list sorely lacked images to go along with the names.

"There really is a lot of stuff, huh…"

"Doctor Babylon was a genius, but-a her organizational skills were subpar… She invented many-a things, and ultimately put them all in the Storehouse. She could've made a lotta dough if she'd spread her creations into the world."

"Doesn't exactly seem like she'd been hurting for cash." I thought back to the golden coins.

"She-a wasn't especially interested in money. The Doctor just-a did what it was she wanted to do." I didn't fully understand the Doctor or why she did the strange things she had done, but I couldn't help but wonder sometimes…

Doctor Babylon had used an artifact to look into the future and see me... And she decided to leave me the floating fortress of Babylon as her legacy. I wondered if there was more to it than that.

"You don't happen to have the item the Doctor used to see into the future in the Storehouse, do you...?"

"To-a see into the future... Mm... You mean the Foresight Jewel? We-a have it, yes." Parshe touched the monolith, and another cube-box sprung up from the floor. It opened up to reveal a beautiful glimmering orb about the size of a volleyball. It was on a masterfully crafted pedestal.

"This is a uh... Foresight Jewel, was it?"

"That's-a right. If you focus your-a magical power, then a person in the future with a similar magical biorhythm to you will be shown in the orb. The person is-a completely random, though. And the future isn't always-a on a stable track. It doesn't-a usually reflect the same person twice, but when the Doctor used it, it always showed you. She must've been-a focusing hard on you." *It was probably because I was the only person it could reflect for her... Though knowing I have a similar biorhythm to that ancient perv isn't really reassuring.*

I tried pouring some of my magic in, but nothing came up. *Huh?* "Is it broken?"

"No. It's-a not broken. It's more likely that a person with your biorhythm won't be born for over five-thousand more years. But of course the future isn't-a fixed. You could always try again later."

"Wait seriously? A person with every magical affinity won't come around for another five-thousand years at least?"

"No. That's-a only one of the factors. Even if-a they have all of the affinities, you won't see them unless you match their magical rhythm closely." *I see... But still, having every magical affinity massively reduces the number of people I can look at. If I had no magical aptitude, I'd probably be able to see multiple people. That sucks.*

I was disappointed since I wanted to look into the future. Parshe mentioned something about being able to roughly estimate how far into the future you looked, so I was hoping to see what became of Brunhild down the line.

"So you just use your magic on it?"

"Yup. It didn't do anything for me." Linze was reading in the living room when I showed up with the Foresight Jewel. What happened next wouldn't be hard to guess.

"It sounds interesting, though. Could I try next?" Elze was on the couch cleaning her gauntlets, but she seemed interested. Yae and Hilde, who were sitting next to her, also seemed curious.

Yumina and Lu entered the room with some tea. Sue was busy at home, and Leen was immersing herself in books at the Library of Babylon.

"R-Right then, let's see…" Linze let her magical power flow into the Jewel, and it suddenly turned a jet black. Little lights flickered inside the orb, sparkling now and then. It was like gazing into space.

The next moment, the image of an old man in a straw hat appeared in the ball. He had a white beard, and was tilling a field. *Huh… What's this?* "Oh… Let-a me tune it…" Parshe lifted up the orb and turned a knob on the back of the pedestal. The image began to fade a bit.

"What's that about?"

"Uhm… It was showing about-a fifty to a hundred years into the future. It seemed-a to be somewhere between Refreese and Regulus. I think." *That's quite far in the future. I wonder if that old man's a little kid right now… Or maybe he hasn't even been born!*

"So… That old man and I have the same biorhythm…?" Linze seemed somewhat disappointed. I could understand, so I was at least a little sympathetic. But at least she had someone tuned to her wavelength.

"I've-a reset the parameters. Now it'll only show up-a to ten years in the future, and the region is limited to-a the local area." Parshe put the Foresight Jewel back down on the table. The discouraged Linze let her shoulders sink a bit, and Elze was the next to touch it.

Once again the beautiful space-like image appeared, and it came into focus on an elderly woman walking through town.

"Huh, is this the castle town?"

"I can see a big clock tower, but… Brunhild doesn't have one of those, does it?"

"Ah… I only saw it for a second, but that was definitely the Silver Moon! It's our town!" Indeed it was. As Yumina said, I had briefly saw the sign for the Silver Moon Inn. Just as I'd thought, it was Brunhild's castle town.

*Huh. Wonder if I'll build a clock tower soon, then… The image is only covering the immediate area around the person, so it's a little hard to get a full view of the place.*

"Uh… D-Did anyone else hear that voice just now? I thought I heard a woman say 'That's a good price.'…" Lu moved slightly closer towards the crystal orb. The woman in the image was buying some apples.

"It's-a making a connection to the targeted person, sometimes it picks up voice. For the most part there's-a too much interference for good audio, but sometimes it comes through well." As everyone listened to Parshe's explanation, the image grew darker until it faded completely.

"Aaaah… The link has-a gone and expired. That-a usually happens a while after you take your hand off."

"We can't see what comes next?"

"That's almost impossible. The target is-a completely random within a scope of ten years, after all." It seemed like the artifact could only be set within a range of decades, it didn't get more precise than that. Even if you were lucky enough to connect to the same person, you'd have to have insane fortune to see a continuation of where you left off last time.

Even Doctor Babylon only saw dotted fragments of my life. Though the fact that she could view me from five-thousand years in the past was incredible enough.

"Who's next?" Yae had no aptitude for magic, so she'd have a broad range of people to potentially synchronize with. Though that came with the disadvantage of it being harder to narrow in on specific individuals. You'd likely look at a different person's future every time you used the orb.

Yae let her magic flow into the crystal ball. Even without any particular aptitude, she still had magic power within her. Enchanted items were originally created for people who couldn't use magic, but they could still channel magic into them.

"Oh… I can see it, I can. Is this… The castle, is it?" There was a maid reflected in the ball. I didn't recognize her face. She was probably someone we'd end up hiring within the next ten years. The young maid walked down the castle hall. She looked to be in her twenties.

"The castle doesn't look much different…"

"Well, it hasn't changed since we built it… So it makes sense it won't change much even after ten years." I grinned slightly at Elze's mutterings, but in turning my head away, I missed what happened next in the vision.

"Hm?!"

"Who is that…?"

"Huh! Wh-What?!" Yae and Yumina stared in surprise. Lu, Linze, and Hilde were also staring down with wonder.

"What was it…? I missed it."

"Ah… U-Uhm, there was a little child. The maid greeted a child and moved on."

"A child?" I turned my head to Linze as she spoke. *A child in the castle, huh… Wait… No way.*

"H-H-Hey! Can't you make the orb pick up on the kid!"

"I-I-It's-a impossible! The target is the maid, I-I'm-a sorry!" Parshe trembled slightly as I grumbled. I was annoyed that I'd missed it.

There was a kid in the castle. It meant that it could've been my kid! Then again, it could've easily been the child of a foreign dignitary. "Was it a boy or a girl?!"

"Uhm… It was a girl… I think?"

"Hm… I believe it was a handsome young man, I do."

"But that long hair… Surely it was a girl."

"Yeah, she was wearing long culotte pants."

"It seemed like she had black hair, too…"

"Th-Th-Then who's the mother!" Everyone went quiet after Hilde's question. Leen and Sue weren't around, but it was possible that we had just seen the daughter (or son?) that they'd eventually bear. Still, knowing who the mother actually was didn't seem like it was possible.

The situation quickly became hectic.

"Hey, Yae! Make the orb show the girl again!"

"I cannot do that, I cannot! I do not control what it shows me, I do not!"

"Aaagh! Y-Yae! Don't let your hand slip! We'll lose connection!"

"I wonder if that was my daughter..."

"Y-Yeah... It's a little scary to think about..."

"I wonder if my child will use a sword like me..."

"Hey, quiet down! I can hear something!" I calmed everyone down and put my finger to my lips. The maid in the crystal ball was talking to a man. He seemed like a co-worker.

"...... --lready ran around over there."

"Good grief. I told the little one not to pester His Majesty... Father or not, he's a very busy man." Everyone's eyes narrowed on me. Welp. That just about confirmed it. I wondered what the future me was doing, though... Shouldn't you be spending time with your family?! "Well, that's it then. We couldn't hear the name... But that child was definitely yours, Touya." I was just upset that I hadn't actually seen the kid with my own two eyes.

The maid bowed her head and left for the kitchen. There were several maids hard at work in the kitchen. The sight wasn't too different to the current state of the place, actually. I was glad I had so many hard workers. ... Though this was a vision of the future, so it would be more apt to say I was glad I was going to have so many hard workers.

"Hey, it's Crea!" Elze pointed to a person reflected in the ball. It was definitely Crea, our current head cook. She looked older, but didn't seem a full ten years older.

"A-Am I not there...?" Lu pouted a little bit. She had a point. Lu spent a lot of time in the kitchen, after all. Sadly it didn't seem like she was in there on this particular day.

Lu's shoulders slumped a little.

"Don't worry, Lu. Why did you want to see yourself so bad, anyway?"

"I wanted you to see the adult me of the future, Touya…"

"Don't be silly. I'll see her gradually, right by my side."

"Ah!" Hilde's sudden exclamation had Lu and I glance towards the crystal ball. *Don't tell me… Not again…*

"J-Just now a little girl left the kitchen with a lunchbox…"

"A-Ah… Sh-She had long, silvery hair…"

"Whaaat?!" Lu let out a shriek. As far as fiancees go, only three had hair you could describe as silvery. Lu, Linze, and Elze. Leen's was more white than anything else.

"Wh-Wh-Where did she go?"

"Ah, she is gone now, she is. She just left the kitchen."

"Go after her!"

"I-I cannot do such a thing…" Lu desperately gazed from the crystal ball to Yae, and then back again. I understood how she felt. I'd missed something again, after all.

"Calm down a little bit… Whose child do you think it was?"

"I-It could have been mine! I-I always thought I'd teach my son or daughter to cook! Th-That's why I'm always working so hard in the kitchen!" It seemed like Lu had been considering more in the long-term than I had been. Still, she had a point. I couldn't imagine Linze or Elze having a kid who spent a lot of time making stuff in the kitchen… I didn't want to imagine what kind of super-spicy horrors Elze would teach her kids to whip up. That being said, they could've been tutored by anyone, so it was hard to say for sure whose child it was.

"We didn't actually see them do any cooking, you know… They might've just been delivering lunch to someone else, or picking up their own."

"Guh… I-I am Lucia Leah Regulus! By my heart, I am sure that my child will be an incredible cook!" Lu spoke firmly, but it came out as more of a mutter. It was ultimately hard to say whether or not Lu's kid would actually be any good in the kitchen. The possibility of Lu teaching Linze's child to cook was always on the table, too.

Still, if she had cooked the lunch she'd left the kitchen with… Who was she delivering it to?

I hoped it was the future me. A handmade lunch from my own daughter. I'd season it with tears of joy as I chowed down.

Or maybe the lunch was for her mother, Lu or otherwise. A gentle, kind child who made lunch for her mom… That's the kind of thing that inspires tears as well.

Or… Maybe she was making lunch for a boy she liked… If she was making lunch for a guy, that'd incite tears in me as well. For another reason entirely.

I had to snap out of that line of thinking. That couldn't be it! Yeah! I wouldn't be letting no stinkin' boys get close to my girls! Hahaha…

As I mused silly things in my head, the maid in the vision spoke with Crea a little and left the kitchen once more.

Suddenly, there was a noise. *Huh?* I looked over to find Yae's head swaying from side to side. Her hand was slipping from the crystal ball. *Crap! Did you run out of magic that fast?!* I caught Yae before she collapsed, but the Foresight Jewel fell from its pedestal and rolled along the floor. Then Parshe fell over. Then Parshe knocked a teapot over.

"Oh, whoa! Excuse-a me!" Parshe reached down to pick up the teapot. It was hot. She dropped it. It fell on the Foresight Jewel. Smash. Crash. Bash. The Pot, along with the Crystal... Crumbled into various pieces.

"AUUUUUUGH?!" Everyone screamed at the same time. It was completely broke. The real tragedy, of course... Was that falling from the pedestal hadn't broken it. It was that damned gynoid!

Everyone gathered around, looking at Parshe in pure disbelief.

*So this is the power of a clumsy shrine maiden, huh...*

"I-I-I-I'm-a sorry!" Parshe immediately brought herself down into a pleading bow. She seemed awfully familiar with that motion. I had a feeling this wasn't the first time she'd ruined absolutely everything.

Still, no use crying over spilled milk. What's done was done. Even though it was broken now, we'd only managed to use the Foresight Jewel thanks to Parshe to begin with.

"Don't worry about it. This was just a peeping Tom's peeking device, anyway."

"B-But..."

"I said it's fine. I don't need to see the future, anyway. The future has infinite possibilities, so it's hard to say if the future we see is the one that'll come to pass anyway." *Your future hasn't been written yet. No one's has. Our future is whatever you make it. So make it a good* one. A white-haired scientist from a movie about a time-traveling car said that once.

"I agree! The future we saw seemed lovely, but let's try and make our own wonderful future together as well."

"I-I agree, I do." Yae, who was still a little woozy despite my use of [**Transfer**] to restore her magic, nodded towards Yumina.

Still, unstable future or not, I was sad I couldn't see my daughter. *I wonder if she's cute and sweet... Yeah, she's definitely cute. Yep. I've decided that just now. She's adorable.*

As I resolutely confirmed the cuteness of my own daughter in my mind, there was a knock at the door. Lapis appeared.

"Sir... The new maids I mentioned the other day are here. I've brought them to greet you. Would you mind meeting them now?"

"Ah, sure thing. I don't mind, bring them in." Living in the castle meant we needed to bring in more staff now and then. Fortunately Lapis had good ties with the maid's guild, and she got us the best staff possible.

At my command, ten new maids filed into the room. But one of the maids in particular stood out. Everyone had the same reaction.

"Aaaaaagh?!"

"Wha-... Eh? Ah...? I-Is there s-something on my face?!" Everyone in the room was pointing and staring at the poor girl.

Her face was decidedly younger, but she was the very image of the maid we'd seen in the crystal ball.

"Amazing..."

"Well... That's a surprise." After everyone settled down and I reassured them, the maids left the room with Lapis.

We were all pretty shocked to see her, despite knowing she was part of an inevitable future that would come.

"Then I wonder if the future we saw is set in stone after all, I do…"

"Hm… Well, it isn't like it was bad or anything." Yae muttered, and Elze returned her own.

It wasn't a bad future at all. It was a future where my children were happy. In fact, I'd call it a very good one indeed.

"Let's do our best, then. To meet our kids in the future." Suddenly, the implications of what I'd said sank in. *Oh crap.* "A-Ah, well… N-Not until we're married… It's a little soon…"

"Y-Yeah, the kids were cute but… I'm not sure if I'm ready for that…"

"E-Even if you want us to do our best, l-let me prepare my heart first…!"

"Wh-Huh?! D-Do our b-best… I-I… I'm not ready for it!" *No, you're getting the wrong idea! I want us to do our best and build a country together! I don't mean we need to start making babies already!* I tried to explain myself, but everyone was far too flustered to listen. I'd sealed my own doom with my flippant comment…

Either way, my future children… It seemed there'd be a long time before I'd get to meet you.

By the way…

I later realized that I could use my Null spell **[Recall]** to find out what my kids looked like. All I needed to do was view the memories of my fiancees.

It was just as I'd thought.

My daughter… Was incredibly cute.

The decision to marry Leen brought a whole lot of trouble with it.

I had to go to Mismede and explain the situation first. I had to promise to take care of appointing a new ambassador for Mismede after informing them that Leen would be stepping out.

Fortunately, or should I say unsurprisingly, His Majesty the Beastking just broke out with his usual hearty laugh and gave me his blessing.

Originally Mismede was a country founded by the seven major demi-human tribes.

In their country, the leader reigns more or less as king, but there's lots of cases in which the patriarchs of each respective tribes stand on equal grounds with him.

It seems opposing Leen's decision as matriarch of the fairy tribe would have been inconceivable for the other tribes.

Just like Leen told me, the other tribes gave their blessings partly due to the fact she wasn't deeply involved in the secrets of the kingdom.

There's many long lived races among them, so most of them have known Leen for a long time.

The chancellor of the kingdom, Glatz, seemed really pleased with the news.

But there was a single exception among all the creatures giving their blessings.

"I'm strongly against this!"

"Eris... I'd have guessed as much." A single girl stood up voicing her obvious displeasure and shock to Leen's decision.

It was Eris of the fairy tribe, court magician of the Kingdom of Mismede.

She looked about 20 years old, pretty different from Leen's petite figure. But being a fairy, she was probably older than she seemed. Her hair was closer to white than platinum blonde, tied up into a ponytail that falls down the height of her shoulders.

Her slender figure was clad in a pretty white blouse adorned with a jeweled ribbon around the chest area. Black stockings and pumps extended from the tight skirt she wore. She was also wearing a set of one bracelet and anklet on her right wrist and ankle respectively.

On top of that she wore an open green robe, and she wielded a staff with some kind of white mark on it that exuded the vibe of intellectualism. There was nothing further from the truth, unfortunately. It was the total opposite of the girl throwing a tantrum in front of everyone right now.

"Why must Miss Leen marry the man from Brunhild?! What of her duties as clan matriarch?!"

"But I haven't done anything here in about 100 years. It won't make much of a difference whether I'm here or not, right? Ah, since we're at it, I'm leaving the position of matriarch to you. Best of luck."

"Are you even listening to me?!" She looked more upset about it all by the second.

I was concerned about dumping so much responsibility on her, but still...

"Besides, why would you ever marry this child?! He won't even last a century! I'm certain he must be wetting his bed every night!"

"That's just nonsense, now." *I guess I can't do anything about being like a baby when compared to centenary fairies, but calling me a child is kinda… I'm kind of the Grand Duke of a Duchy, come on.*

"But age is just a number. That doesn't have anything to do with love, does it now? That's why your partner is…"

"N-N-N-Never mind that! Anyhow, I won't accept this! I'm not about to hand Miss Leen over to some stranger!"

"He's not a stranger. I've told you a thousand times already. He's the Grand Duke of Brunhild."

"Why you little…!" She was a real handful. I managed to see Paula by Leen's feet shrugging in resignation. It was a real fuss.

"You might have merits enough to take Miss Leen's hand in marriage, but I won't accept it until you prove yourself."

"How can I do that?"

"A trial! If you can overcome the trial of the fairies I'll allow you to take Miss Leen's hand in marriage! But if you fail, the engagement will have to be called off!" Things went south pretty quick… But it wasn't like I could run away. I didn't know what she wanted me to do, but I resolved to try.

"The fairies take pride in their magic prowess! We can't allow someone without that gift to marry our leader! You need control of the highest order over magic. I'll have you show me your power!" The place chosen for our match was the arena standing behind the Mismede Palace. It was the same place I had my fight with the Beastking. It was as big as I remembered.

I took a look at the stands and found there were actually people watching us. Maybe they caught wind of our match and came out of curiosity. Naturally, the king was on a special seat with an entertained look on his face. *Have you considered doing your job, dear king?*

"What am I supposed to control?"

"I shall strike you with magic! You'll have to cancel it out! The attribute of the magic doesn't matter! But it can't be either too weak or too strong! If my magic touches you you'll lose! Ah, barrier spells are prohibited, just so you know!" *Isn't the whole "I can choose any amount of power and attribute" part kind of unfair? Well whatever. I can negate attacks pretty easily.*

Well, it was true you wouldn't be able to cancel your enemy's magic unless you can match their strength, but there were other ways to negate damage.

"So, in short, it'll be okay as long as I negate your magic before it gets to me, right?"

"Hmph! Enjoy the time you have to bluff while you can! Let's start! **Come forth, Fire! Crimson Javelin of Flames: [Fire Spear]!**" A flame spear came out of the staff she was wielding.

*Oooh... I'd heard fairies weren't very good at using fire magic, so I didn't think fairies besides Leen could use it.*

But I guess this wasn't the moment to be amazed. I conjured up my own magic to negate hers.

"**[Absorb]!**" The fire spear dissipates and disappeared before it could hit me.

"Huh?! What's that?!"

"It's one of my null spells. It's magic that allows me to transform your magic into magical power, is there a problem?"

"Didn't I say I wanted to see your control!? Sucking it up is foul play!"

"Uh... But you said the attribute didn't matter."

"No null magic!" *Tsk. You do need control to manage using null magic like I can, you know?* "So you have the gall to try and make a fool out of me... I'll show you! **Thunder, Heed my Call: [Thunder Spear]!**" "Alright, geez! [Thunder Spear]!" The clash of the two spears echoed across the arena like a thunderclap, creating a sphere of energy right in the center of it. They canceled each other out and vanished.

"Guh! **Pierce, o ice! Frozen Point: [Ice Needle]!**" "[Ice Needle]..." Same result, the icy needles canceled each other out in the middle of the arena. It was easy to cancel a spell out by using the same spell. Although it wouldn't be that difficult to do the same with opposing elements either. She was pretty simple to read.

**"Come forth, o Light! Shining Duet: [Light Arrow]!"** "[Light Arrow]." The light arrows canceled each other out just like the icy needles did.

After that the same happened with some fire spears and stone bullets.

"Wait just a minute! How many elements can you handle!? Six if we count the null magic?! Are you the same as Miss Leen?!"

"Eeh, not really..."

"Eris, he can use all the elements. That makes him better than me."

"Excuse me!?" Her eyes went wide as saucers. It seemed like Eris could use fire, water, wind, earth, and light. Having aptitude for two elements was enough of a feat. Linze and Yumina could use three. The matriarch of the fairies, Leen, could use six. The fact that this girl could use five was more than amazing in its own right.

"Why you…! Don't get carried away!" She extended her hands and started gathering magical power. Oh? **"Come forth, Fire! Crimson Duet: [Fire Arrow]! Come forth, Water! Feel My Blade, Both Cold and Clear: [Aqua Cutter]!"** She conjured two spells at once and sent them flying towards me. *Oh, so she can cast two types of magic at the same time?* **"Ugh… [Fire Arrow]. [Aqua Cutter]."** I cast two spells at the same time just like her, and they canceled each other out.

Her face was overcome by surprise, but it didn't take long for that to be washed away by a raging red flush. Followed by a nonstop barrage of magic and angry prattling.

"Take this! And this! You puny little…!"

"Whoa! There! Hah!" I made sure to confirm the order of the random magic she hurled my way, and countered it with magic of the same type. Somehow, the more flustered she got only made me feel calmer. So much in fact I started thinking about how nice it would be if she threw a feint or something…

"Guh… Hahh… Hahh…" Eris looked unsteady, she was leaning on her staff for support. Her legs were buckling, I wondered if she was alright. Leen, the referee, raised her hand.

"That's it. Eris ran out of magical power."

"I can keep going!"

"It'd be nice if you stopped being so stubborn." Paula walked to the spot Eris was standing and poked her legs. It didn't take a second for her to fall down to her knees. She was on her last legs for sure.

"Ugh…"

"See? Running out of magic is a matter of life and death for magicians. I told you to always keep at least ten percent of your magic even in emergency cases, didn't I?"

"I-I'm sorry…" Leen used [**Transfer**] to give the weakened Eris some power back.

She got up immediately and stared daggers at me.

"This is not over! You're sorely mistaken if you think magic prowess alone is enough to make you a fitting partner for Miss Leen!" *What now…? She's really pretty, but everything else about her is a disappointment. It feels like I'm dealing with a little kid or something.*

"Tsk, you were thinking something rude just now, weren't you?"

"Hm? Nope." She was sharper than she looked, at least.

"This place is called the Lost Forest. It's said that you'll be lost forever if you can't read the forest's heart. 'Tis but a trifling task for us fairies, but can a simple human go into this forest and come out?" She crossed her arms and looked at me arrogantly.

We were in a forest south of Mismede, close to the Sea of Trees.

The forest was a territory that belonged to the Fairy Tribe.

Eris was so smug and self-assured because it was easy for outsiders to get lost. Unless one made a bond with the forest or got the help of a fairy, they'd be unable to escape.

It was actually forbidden to enter due to a matter of public safety.

"Getting cold feet? I don't mind if you wanna stop here. In exchange, I don't want to see you near Miss Leen ever again."

"Eris, enough of this." Leen sighed at Eris' cheap provocation. Once again, the stuffed bear, Paula, shrugged in resignation.

"I'll go in if that's what you want. How do you want this done?"

"There's a giant apple tree in the middle of the forest. Take a fruit and come back here. If you can even get there in the first place, that is. Well, if you haven't managed to come out in two days, I'll go to your rescue." *Rescue, huh... That part about coming to my rescue sounds a bit suspicious... ah well.*

"Just so you know, you can't use magic inside this forest. No transportation or searching magic either, you hear me?"

"Ugh." *And here I was about to use the map to find the apple and come back using a portal; she shot me right down. Tsk.*

"Are you sure you'll be okay? You don't have to go along with everything Eris says, you know." Leen spoke with a slight frown on her face. She seemed worried about me.

"It's fine, honestly. I'll manage somehow even without magic."

"Hmph! I hope you're having a fun time trying to show off, because it won't last long!" Eris spoke again, smug and confident in herself. I wasn't really trying to sound cool or anything, though.

*Well, I guess talking won't do me much good, so I better wrap this up as soon as I can.*

"Alright then, I'm going." I took my first step into the lost forest and waved them off.

*... One Hour Later...*

"Why?! How did you manage it so fast?! Who's that girl?!" Eris screamed at me as I munched an apple.

There was a green-haired girl with a puzzled expression by my side. Her long hair flowed like a waterfall of emeralds. It matched her green dress perfectly. The confusion was clear in her jade eyes as she looked at the girl ranting in front of her.

"I was wondering if my voice would make it to anyone since the place's so close to the sea of trees, she really saved me."

"Oh no, I didn't do anything... Heh... Umm, is she okay?"

"Don't ignore me! That's why I asked who she was!" I ignored her on purpose, and wouldn't you guess, she got mad again. *Maybe I'm teasing her a little too much. Sorry, Eris.*

"She's a forest spirit. One of the avatars of the great tree that rules over the sea of trees. Everything went smoothly when I asked her to guide me."

"Huh?"

"Mister Touya is a patron of the sea of trees. This bit of help is nothing of importance. Besides…" *Whoa there, don't go revealing my divinity…* I got her attention and put my index finger over my mouth to keep the spirit from talking any further.

Leen didn't miss the gesture, she put her hands over her hips and let out an exasperated sigh. Even Paula, who was standing by her feet, copied her.

"Darling, I don't think using a spirit as guide is appropriate."

"It felt more like mediation rather than guidance, really. Something along the lines of not letting the lost forest get in my way." Besides, the forest's heart Eris was talking about in the first place means the spirits that lived in it. The great tree spirit was the same as the small spirits that lead the people who enter the forest astray.

Basically, they had freedom to do as they pleased. The fact they lead people astray is probably due to their role as protectors of the apple tree. It seems like a place for all the little spirits to have fun and relax, after all.

The fairies were friends to the forest spirits, so they weren't taken astray by them.

"Why does a forest spirit have to guide you?! It's inexcusable, isn't it!? Come on now, admit it!"

"Eris, you're aware of the aggressive stance you're taking against the leader of a whole nation, aren't you? This person is the Grand

Duke of Brunhild. You're Mismede's court magician. One step in the wrong direction can mean the end of diplomatic relationships, you know that, don't you? You'd do well to think before talking when you have part of the weight of the whole country on your shoulders."

"Uuuh…" Eris flinched a bit when the person she respected so much talked to her like that. Well, I (and probably Mismede's king) didn't mind so much, but that may not apply for the rest of the nations. It'd be bad if she offended another nation in public.

"W-Well be thankful you got lucky enough to meet a spirit! If you hadn't, you'd have gotten lost and you would have begged and cried for my help!!!"

"Yeah, yeah. I get it. Is it over now?"

"Of course not! Don't think you're even remotely a match for Miss Leen! Even if she approves, you don't have approval from the clan's elders!"

"The elders of the fairy tribe?" I looked back at Leen, and she had an unusually troubled expression on her face. I wondered what was up. "The elders… I'm sure it'll be fine. I wrote a letter to them explaining the circumstances." Something seemed off. She was frowning. Her usual cute face seemed troubled. "What's the deal with the elders, are they higher in status than you?"

"In a sense. The elders are successive in our clan. It is their job to guide the current leaders and shape their direction of the fairy tribe."

"You never really spoke about them." Leen's voice fell to a low murmur. From what I understood, the tribe elders would guide the new generation before passing on their titles to their successors.

"Miss Leen! They simply didn't reply because they didn't feel the need to! You've done much for our people." That seemed right. As far as I knew, Leen had increased the standing of the fairies in Mismede by a whole bunch.

"You still must meet with them for approval!"

"No, that isn't necessary." I looked to Leen.

"Well, I think I should probably meet with them. Even if they don't have a lot of spare time, it's important."

"Hmph. Then you wish to meet with them? The elders have recently been playing this game called shogi, though. They haven't had much time on their hands." Eris' words surprised me. I didn't realize shogi had even spread that far. But then again, Olba was my main distributor, and he was from Mismede... So it wasn't all that odd.

"If you wish to meet with the elders of the fairy village, I can take you." The forest spirit spoke up. That certainly was convenient.

"Thanks, spirit."

"...If you insist." Leen didn't seem all that amused. She must have really had a disdain for her tribe's elders. I wondered if they were really as much trouble as she was suggesting, though.

Either way, I wanted to do this by the book. If I was to marry Leen, I wanted to let everyone related to her know it.

The forest spirit touched a large tree nearby, and the trunk opened up to form a passageway.

"This will take you to the elders of the fairy village. By all means, please make use of it."

"Gotcha!" Eris leaped through the passage. Paula skipped onwards too, tugging at Leen's arm. I followed behind them, and it closed behind us.

"Hm...?" Eventually the tunnel ended and we came out into the open. We were still in the forest, of course.

There were lots of houses in the trees. They looked like log cabins. Bridges joined all the trees together, too. And naturally there were people on those bridges and in those houses, too.

Flowers and grass swayed in the breeze. It was a beautiful place indeed.

A man walking nearby took notice, and he looked over towards us. He had insect-like wings on his back, much like Leen's. He looked like a twenty-year-old man.

"Huh? Leen's here?"

"Ah... Sureigis... It's been a while." Leen smiled softly. He looked pretty young, so I didn't think he was one of the elders. Then again, he could've been... Fairies stopped aging after a fixed point. So he could've been really, really old.

"I'll say! It's been like four-hundred years! Ever since you skipped town after blowing away Ermela's house..."

"I don't remember trivial things like that." Leen leered slightly at Sureigis. *Wh... She blew away someone's house?!*

"My my... The villainous fairy Leen has finally shown up to face down the elders... Have you finally come to accept your... role... as matri...arch...?" The man's voice gradually slowed and became quieter. Leen was staring him down, flicking fireballs between her fingers as if they were simple toys. Paula was shivering in some pattern of faux-fear.

I remembered Leen being good with fire magic, which was rare for a fairy. "Goodness, Sureigis... You want to be cooked that badly?"

"N-No! A-Ah, look at the time! I-I better go inform everyone of your arrival, hahaah!" Sureigis ran off like the wind was carrying him. He sure could run...

Leen let out a little sigh. As she did, the fireballs vanished.

She got a little bit embarrassed when she noticed me staring at her.

"Ah... W-Well... There was an incident some t-time ago, I... I was just a child! Aaagh! I-I'm not so hot-headed now, I promise! That was the past, the past!" Leen's cheeks turned red as she got herself all flustered. I wondered if that was why she was reluctant to meet the elders. Perhaps they only knew Leen as some rampant troublemaker.

She turned her face away and attempted to compose herself. She usually wore such a cool and calm expression, so seeing her like this was a rare treat.

"D-Don't laugh…"

"Sorry, sorry. You shouldn't get worked up, though. Everyone did stupid things as a kid. Even I did."

"Hmph. From my perspective you're still a kid."

"Oh hush it. I mean it, I'm much more mature than I used to be. When I was thirteen and fourteen, I was especially troublesome…" It was funny to think about… That was only a year or two before God had sent me to this new world… But it felt like a lifetime ago.

I used to mess around with motorcycle gangs, and I helped ruin the social life of a sketchy substitute teacher who was trying to make a girlfriend out of one of his students…

Thinking back, I did some reckless crap. Even if I had good intentions, there were better ways to go about it… I wasn't entirely sure how much I'd matured, really… But I knew I was a different man in this world.

"My feelings for you won't change, Leen. In fact, I'm glad for the past you had and the past I had. Without either, we'd have never met."

"Hehe… I… I like that… Thank you, darling." Leen gently hugged me. That was rare. When the other fiancees were around, Leen typically stayed in the background. Seemed like she took her chances whenever she could get them.

"What the heck are you two doing?! Quit hugging in public! Gross! Losers!" Eris ruined the moment by physically prying Leen and I apart. Paula gently hugged my leg. *Th-Thanks…*

"Wow, it's really Leen..."

"Long time no see, are you well?"

"Nena, Ati... I'm glad to see you." A girl who looked to be about twenty, and a girl who looked to be about eight both ran over towards us.

Nena looked like a typical little girl you'd find in a village. Her hair was white and done up in braids that flowed down her front. I wondered if this child was an elder.

Ati, on the other hand... Well, she was as flat as a board. If her hair wasn't long she'd have easily been mistaken for a man. She seemed aloof, kind of like a stern older sister.

"We heard the news! Congratulations!"

"Is the rumor true? We heard you'd caught yourself a little boytoy."

"Gh-! How do you know already?! We only just told the Beastking!" Leen looked completely taken aback, and Ati spoke up in response.

"Heh... Elders have their own information sources, you know. Everyone already knows."

"What?!" Leen seemed a little annoyed. But, before we knew it, we'd been whisked off to a grand banquet alongside the elders of the village.

"Let's hear it for Leen and the Grand Duke of Brunhild! Cheers!"

"Cheers!" Fireflies illuminated the night like magical lanterns as I greeted each elder one-by-one. Leen followed, and I ended up hearing many stories about her past. This often ended in Leen getting embarrassed or irritated, though. It was funny.

Amazingly, everyone was happy, and we celebrated all night long. Nobody objected to the marriage. Well. Nobody except Eris, who was still grumbling in the corner.

"Hrmph…" Apparently everything had been smoothed out for a while. The elders had long-forgotten the fuss that made Leen leave the village.

"Eris…"

"Miss Leen…" Leen went over to talk with Eris. She was trouble, but she still cared about Leen a lot. They were family, in a sense.

"Come on now… Isn't this good enough? You know I'm no fool… Don't you trust in me? Hey, Eris… You know… Your approval would mean more to me than any of the elders."

"I… I… Don't want you to leave us, Leen… Everyone leaves… And we finally formed a nation for people like us… It's only been around for twenty years, and… And you're leaving!" Leen sighed, then gave Eris a little hug.

"Hey now… This is my home, Eris. And I trust you dearly with the responsibilities. I'm giving this to you because of what you mean to me, alright? You're the matriarch, and you'll be wonderful. Someday you'll pass it on, as well… We pass on our feelings that way. I'll watch over you, and I'll guide you too. Just like the elders do."

"Miss Leen…"

"Please take care, Eris… You mustn't get headstrong. You're in an important position now, and you must lead our people with care and grace. Promise me you'll stand up against injustice. In or out of Mismede. If you don't… I'll… Pinch your nose!"

"Gah!" Leen grinned as she gently squeezed Eris' nose. Paula, who was at Leen's feet, gradually shuffled off to do her own thing.

After a while, Eris came over to me. She pointed a finger in my direction.

"You… I… I reluctantly admit that you mean much to Miss Leen! But know that I will come down upon you if you fail to make her happy!"

"That goes without saying… But I promise. I'll make Leen as happy as can be."

"H-Hmph!" Eris shuffled off with a little blush on her face. I thought I caught her smiling as she went back to the elders.

"Man, I'm tired…"

"Well hey… We got her blessing." Leen sat down next to me. We had gone through a lot, but we'd finally sorted it all out.

"I wish she'd just been honest from the beginning. That girl has a troublesome personality… But her heart's in the right place." Leen smiled and sighed. I definitely agreed with that. I wondered if she'd be alright as the new matriarch.

"I asked the elders to watch her closely. What comes next is for Eris and the fairies to determine, not us." Leen rested her head on my shoulder. I was a little embarrassed, but… We were engaged, so it was fine.

Eris had accepted it, and so had the others.

《…… My liege, do you hear me? Are you getting this?》 "Huh… What's going on…" I could hear Kohaku's voice in my head. I wondered if something had happened. 《Uh… Hold on, how do I do this again… Ah. Right! Yeah, I hear you!》 《Touya! Where are you right now?》 Yumina's voice came through in my head, and my blood ran cold.

*Oh shit. I didn't tell them I'd be out late! I've gone and done it again!* "A-Ah… Yumina… Uhm. Right now I'm just at the village of the fairies with Leen." 《Alright, thanks. We should all go there sometime, too! I hope you're having fun. It's just getting late, so don't forget to keep us in the loop next time.》 *Goddammit. I really need to remember the fact that I can use telepathic messaging…* Paula was shivering like crazy. *C-Calm down, you're okay…*

《Anyway, I need to tell you-》 "It's okay! We're coming home right now! I'll be there in thirty seconds!" I didn't want another lecture, so I cut off the transmission, told the elders that we had to leave, grabbed Leen, grabbed Paula, whipped open a **[Gate]** and hurtled through at mach speed.

"...I wish you the best!" Just as we went through the portal, I heard Eris' parting words. She seemed a little drunk, but... The two of us smiled.

"Yes, let's be happy together, darling..."

"That's the plan." Paula mimed a little giggle as I replied to Leen.

"Now what could this be?" Yumina found something strange as we were searching through the artifacts in Babylon's Storehouse (with the exception of any dangerous and/or sexual artifacts).

Okay, so while it was indeed strange, I knew exactly what it was with just a cursory glance. It was a cube with its six sides each marked with a different number of stars (☆), from one star to six. No matter how you looked at it, it was a die.

It seemed that dice existed in this world, too. Except they weren't called dice, but "dicen" instead.

And they were used as a divination tool to make decisions with the guidance of the spirits rather than a random number generator for games and the like.

"It's quite big for a dicen, isn't it?" Lu muttered after taking a look at the die Yumina was holding. It was indeed quite big. Dice were usually about one or two centimeters wide, even over here. But the one Yumina had was about thirty centimeters wide. It was comically huge as far as dice go.

"Is this perhaps another artifact?"

"I'd assume so, since it's in the Storehouse and all, but..." Elze and Linze paused their sorting of the weapons and weapon accessories and came over this way. Oh, and if you were wondering, I had already unlocked all the chests.

Yae and Hilde were carrying over the sorted chests, but also paused to send a curious look this way.

"Find any spec sheets?"

"No... not at all. This is all we found." All of the artifacts stored in the Storehouse were contained in cubic chests. The artifacts, including the blueprints, were all compressed and stored similarly through a technique similar to my [**Storage**] spell.

Without the spec sheets, we'd have no idea how to use any of the artifacts.

Oh, and by the way, the spec sheets were written in Partheno, which I could inexplicably read. According to Parshe, the inscription magic and translation magic infused within was able to directly transmit the meaning into my brain upon sight... or something like that. Anyway, I was just glad I didn't have to use [**Reading**] to read it.

"I guess the easiest way to find out would be to just ask the manager, but... where'd Parshe go, anyway?" Parshe, the manager of the Storehouse, was nowhere to be found. Could've sworn she was here a second ago. Elze had just the answer I was looking for.

"Oh, Parshe went to go deliver an artifact to the alchemy lab. She said it'd be useful as a compounding tank or something." A compounding tank? Like for pharmaceuticals or something? The Storehouse was Babylon's treasure trove. It was filled with items that'd be useful for other buildings on Babylon, so there'd be no problem redistributing them, but...

"Let's just hope she doesn't trip and break it..." That's the klutz of a manager we're talking about. Pretty sure I wasn't the only one who was slightly worried.

"Hey, get back to work everyone! We want to get this over with at some point in time, don't we?" Leen's voice came echoing down from the Storehouse loft. Paula was up there with her hands placed angrily on her hips, too.

"If the Library is home to the crystallization of ancient knowledge, then the Storehouse is home to the crystallization of ancient technology." Leen was quite keen to see all things to be seen, it would seem.

"Since it's a dicen, it's meant to be thrown to decide something, right? Lemme see it for a sec, Yumina."

"Ah, Sue! Wait…!" Before I could stop her, Sue snatched the die from Yumina and tossed it into the air.

Though it may have been a die in shape, it was an artifact made by Doctor Babylon herself. There was no telling what would happen. In fact, I was sure that something would happen! The die bounced off the white floor of the Storehouse before rolling and stopping on one.

"Ngh. That's bad luck." Did I mention that dicen were fortune-telling tools in this world? Apparently six meant excellent luck, and one meant bad luck.

Sue furrowed her eyebrows and not a second later, the die started to make a low whistling noise… when suddenly, we all got sucked in towards it. *What the hell?*

"Kyah?"

"W-what's going on?!"

"My liege?!" Right before my eyes, Yumina, Elze, and Yae got sucked into the "one" star on the top of the die.

One by one, Linze, Lu, Leen, Sue, and Hilde got sucked in like a vacuum cleaner, leaving Paula flailing around frantically before I got sucked into the die as well.

"Dammit! See?! Of course something like this would happen!" I cursed the name of the genius doctor from five millennia ago as my consciousness faded away.

"Oww... ...Where am I?" I woke up in a place that resembled Babylon's garden. The flowers and the trees were bright and lively. Everyone else was sitting around the lawn. Thank goodness. It looked like everyone was safe. But still, where were we...?

"Touya, look at that."

"Huh? ...What is that...?" Yumina pointed up to the blue sky dotted with clouds, where Paula's giant, translucent face peered down at us.

Up above was a faint five-pointed star pattern. Don't tell me...

"Are we inside the die?" Well, I did see everyone get sucked in, so I had a feeling that was the case.

"Teleportation magic brought us to a reality marble... perhaps. It might be similar to the hangar. Paula?! Can you hear us?" Leen shouted at the giant Paula in the sky. Paula nodded and raised both fists in the air.

"We're safe! And sorry, but could you head to the alchemy lab and tell Parshe what happened?" Paula nodded again before disappearing. She probably went to go find Parshe. Who knows if we'll be safe, though... It's not like she could talk... Well, I'm sure she'll be able to get the gist across with some charades. I hope.

"Anyway, what exactly could this artifact be, I wonder?"

"An enemy-trapping artifact... perhaps?" Yae and Hilde wondered aloud as they surveyed the area.

We were indeed trapped in here, but... I just remembered what this situation reminded me of. It was like the magic gourd from Journey to the West that the Gold Horn and Silver Horn Kings got sucked into after responding to their names. It was like that, but... We didn't respond to our names.

*How did Wukong escape from the gourd after he got sucked in, again?* "Excuse me, Touya... Can we not use your teleportation magic to escape?"

"Oh, right. That." I couldn't help but clap my hands after Lu pointed out the obvious.

*Why didn't I think of that...? Wow, how embarrassing.* I cleared my throat, activated **[Gate]** and... nothing happened. "What's wrong?"

"I can't open a **[Gate]** right now. In fact, my magic's just fizzling out."

"Huh?!" Leen and Linze tried using magic just to make sure, but their magic too fizzled out, unable to activate. Seemed like magic couldn't be used here. "Nope. Teleportation magic won't do you any good here."

"Wh-who's there?!" The voice came from midair, where a woman appeared, sitting in a chair.

She wore glasses and a white coat as she smoked something like a cigarette. Her eyes looked languid, but a bold smile adorned her face.

"Dr. Babylon..."

"Huh, that's her?!" Yumina's eyes popped.

That was her, beyond a shadow of a doubt. She was a perfect match to the 3D model of her that Cesca showed me the first night I became the master of the Garden. Oh, on second thought, this could just be another 3D model...

"Welcome to Babylon World. Allow me to entertain you with some momentary amusement. The rules of this game are quite simple. Just roll the dicen and advance that number of spaces. It's that simple." A map demarcated with square spaces from Start to Finish appeared beside Dr. Babylon. And just like the Storehouse spec sheets, the labels on the map appeared to be encoded with translation magic, as I could read them even though they were written in Partheno.

Sure, I could read it, but… umm…

"What is this, Snakes and Ladders…?" Not only did dicen exist five millennia ago, but so did Snakes and Ladders, I guess. Seems it just fell out of fashion these days for some reason. But anyway, that's not the problem.

"Hunt five goblins?"

"Gather ten stones…"

"Do an impression of a king ape?"

"What might these inscriptions on the spaces mean?" It didn't seem to click with the others, but I knew exactly what was going on. When you landed on a space, you had to do what was written there! "You have three hours. If you reach the goal within that time limit, I shall return you to where you came from. But even if you don't reach the goal in three hours, you'll still be returned to where you came from, so don't worry."

"So I guess we're not trapped here forever." Linze breathed a sigh of relief. Even if we don't reach the goal…? Sounds kinda fishy. There's no way the doctor would make a child's game mere child's play.

After I gave her a dubious glare, the 3D model of Dr. Babylon predictably continued to speak.

"But if you lose, I'll strip you all of your clothes as a penalty. And I do mean all your clothes, including your underwear!"

"Ugh, you're the worst!!!" Everyone cast their voices in unison, echoing the cast die.

So in other words, if we don't reach the goal in three hours, we'll be kicked out of here butt-naked? "What?! Are you sure this person's really *the* Dr. Babylon?!"

"I'm afraid so…" I gave the enraged Lu the cold, hard truth. I couldn't tell you how many times I'd thought the exact same thing. The doctor was the type of whimsical person to follow through on her impulses, no matter how stupid they might be. The fact that she was a genius only made matters worse. She undoubtedly must've been a headache to everyone around her.

"Now let the games begin. See you in three hours." The doctor's midair 3D model disappeared and a die the same size as the one we got sucked into fell down onto the ground.

And at the same time, the remaining time appeared next to the map and began counting down.

"Wh-what do we do?"

"We do what we gotta do, or we'll be stripped naked?"

"It wouldn't be a problem if it were just us, but…" Yae, Elze, and Hilde all shot their glances at me. Well, yeah. I knew exactly what they wanted to say.

"Darling, you're not thinking of losing on purpose, are you?"

"…No… Of course not…"

"You hesitated just now."

"You looked away just now." As soon as I answered Leen's question, Yumina and Lu immediately shot me down with their double princess glare. *Just let it slide, Touya. Just let it slide.*

Obviously, I had no intention of hindering everyone else… but I had to admit, I was thinking if we lost, we lost. Even if we got out of there butt naked, I could just use [**Mosaic**] to cover our bits.

"U-Uhm… time's ticking away…" Linze snapped everyone's attention back to the map's timer. We had already wasted three minutes.

"Not good. We can't waste time or we'll be kicked out of here naked."

"So anyway, we just gotta roll that dicen, right? Go?" Sue tossed the giant die. It bounced two or three times as it rolled. It landed on three.

"Ah, the marks on the map…" The star mark on the starting line began to advance on the map. To show us which space we're supposed to land on, I guess. And sure enough, the star mark stopped exactly three spaces later.

The next moment, the die disappeared and our surroundings transformed into a forest.

"Hunt five silbirds…?" I read aloud the text written on the space we stopped on, and right on cue, a number of squawking silver-winged birds started flying out from the trees.

"I guess those are silbirds?"

"Are they real?" Yumina dubiously asked as she gazed at the silver birds fluttering about the sky. I thought they were probably 3D models… or some sort of summoning magic, but…

"Anyway, let's just follow the instructions." I unsheathed Brunhild in Gun Mode and set my sights on the silver birds fluttering in the air.

I fired two shots. Pew, pew! The first shot missed. The second hit the silbird, but instead of falling to the ground, it unexpectedly just faded away in the air. Even though I shot regular bullets. Not magic bullets, just plain old regular bullets.

"I guess it was just a model after all. Looks like they're set to disappear when hit."

"Touya, allow me." Yumina took out the Colt Army Model 1860 I'd made for her from her ring's [**Storage**] and set her sights. I had modified the gun's barrel and grip to make it easier for Yumina to hold, so it looked quite different from the original model.

Yumina pulled the trigger in rapid succession, annihilating three silver birds as they flew. *Amazing.*

Yumina shot down the last remaining bird with her keen eye as well.

And at the same time, a chime bonged and the giant die reappeared on the ground.

"Looks like we cleared the requirements."

"Guess that means it wants us to continue." I nodded at Linze.

*Roll the die and do what's written on the space you land on. Clear the requirements and you can advance. Exactly like Snakes and Ladders.* Except we had no opponent, so we had no turns off to relax.

"Who's gonna roll next?" Sue asked as she picked up the die. I wasn't sure it mattered who rolled the die, but we decided an order and had Elze roll next.

"What's written on the next few spaces?"

"Let's see… Sing a song, Advance two spaces, Laugh for an entire minute, Do a thousand pushups, Talk like a cat, Wear the provided wig… None of these look any good."

Lu frowned as she read the map. *Well, that's the doctor for you. 'Advance two spaces.' leading right to 'Do a thousand pushups.' is just plain cruel.*

"Well, I'll give it a roll." Elze tossed the die with a yelp. The die tumbled on the ground and stopped on six.

"Yay!" Elze did a fist pump. She realized that bigger numbers meant reaching the goal faster. Which was great and all, but…

The map indicator rhythmically advanced spaces one by one.

Once the indicator stopped on the sixth space, our surroundings changed once more. And once again, the die disappeared.

We appeared to be inside a castle's dressing room this time. Racks of clothes surrounded us on all sides.

The walls on either side were full-length mirrors, and there was a desk in the center of the room. A box with a large hole cut out of the top sat atop it. There was something written on the side of the box facing us.

"The instructions on the space say to 'wear the provided wigs'… But I don't see any wigs anywhere."

"Maybe they're inside the box? There's something written on it at least."

"Let's see here. 'Every person must stick their hand into the box and wear whatever they pick out.' Wait, does that mean we have to, too?" Leen read the words on the box, a hint of incredulity creeping into her voice. She'd expected only the person who'd rolled the die would have to participate, but it seemed this was something we'd all be doing. It appeared we'd be sharing our fates for the duration of this game.

"Well…we might as well do this in dice-rolling order. Elze, you're first."

"Huh, me?!" Though the hole was rather wide, we couldn't see inside the box. There must have been some kind of magical effect placed on it or something to hide its contents.

Elze timidly lowered her hand into the box, grabbed something, and pulled it out.

At first glance, it looked to be a brimless black hat, but...

"This is a wig?"

"Perhaps...something will happen if you put it on?" Elze hesitantly put the hat on at her younger sister's urging. A second later, her hairstyle was transformed.

*I see now. S-So this is how it works. Heh.*

"Ahahahahaha! No way! I'm sorry Elze, this is just too good!!!"

"W-What?!" I couldn't stop laughing. The wig had turned Elze's hairdo into a crew cut. I had no idea how it had managed to make her long hair disappear, but it had. *Illusion magic, perhaps? Bahahaha, I'm laughing too hard to think straight!* The others all turned away, doing their best to hide their laughter.

Confused, Elze turned to one of the mirrors to see what she looked like. "Are you serious?!" Elze screamed as she saw her reflection.

She tried to take the cap off her head, but it seemed glued on. I suspected that her hairstyle would remain this way until we rolled the die again, or until some time passed.

"Jeez! You guys hurry up and pull your wigs out too! Touya, you're next!"

"Wait, I'm next?!" Urged onward by Elze, I stuck my hand into the box and pulled out a golden cap. *This... looks flashy.*

"Hurry up and put it on!"

"Alright, alright..." I turned around and put the cap on. When I turned back, everyone burst into laughter. What kind of hairstyle did this wig give me? I looked over at the mirror and saw a blonde, twin-tailed me staring back. Are you kidding me...

"Now we match, Darling. Heh." Leen walked up behind me and patted me on the shoulder. This isn't the kind of matching I wanted! "Oh whatever! Everyone, hurry up and get your wigs so we can get out of here! Who's next?!" Trying to hide my embarrassment, I hurried the others onward. Everyone ended up with a ridiculous hairstyle. Linze had ringlet curls, Yumina had an afro, Lu had dreadlocks, Leen had a pompadour, Yae had a mohawk, Hilde had a lion's mane, and Sue ended up looking half-bald.

Out of all of them, mine might actually have been the least ridiculous. Though I still would have preferred Elze's crew cut wig. Actually, the hairstyles themselves weren't ridiculous, it was just that none of them fit. There were some people who could really pull off a pompadour or mohawk.

And Linze's ringlet curls actually looked kind of good on her. If she had a more domineering personality, they would have fit her perfectly. As it was, they kind of clashed with her quiet demeanor.

Once we all had our wigs on, the dicen fell to the ground again.

Linze picked it up and threw it with all her might. It landed on four. The star mark moved another four spaces forward.

"This one says...'Everyone say aloud the color of your underwear.' Wait whaaaaaat?!" Linze screamed hysterically. The girls all looked at each other in shock. I let out a wild cheer inside my heart, but kept my expression perfectly neutral.

"Hey Linze! Why'd you have to land there, of all places?!"

"You're scaring me, sis! Don't glare at me with that hairdo!" Linze raised her arms to shield herself from Elze's menacing stare. The crew cut made her twice as scary.

"We simply have to announce the color of our underwear? Very well, mine is white." Sue casually announced her underwear's color. There's a lot I wanted to say about her nonchalance when it came to underwear, but now wasn't the time. I figured I might as well use this opportunity to mention mine too.

"I guess I'll say mine too. My underwear's black. Alright, next." Since I was standing next to Sue, I more or less established that we'd go down in line.

Next was Yae, who was standing on my other side. She was looking awfully flustered, which would have been cute if she didn't have a mohawk.

"Hm?" Mine and Sue's wigs had vanished. Ah, I get it now. Once we clear the next event, the previous event's effects vanished.

"So they'll go away once we say our underwear's color."

"I wonder if that means they won't vanish if we lie about it." Yae muttered, looking depressed. Had Yae been hoping to get away with a lie? Knowing her, we would have been able to see through it right away.

Normally I'd have said no one would be that cruel, but knowing the doctor she might really do it.

I was wearing black boxers, so my answer certainly hadn't been a lie. I'd gotten them from Zanac's shop, and they were a copy of the underwear I'd been wearing when I'd first come to this world.

"M-My underwear also happens to be… wh-wh… ngh… r-red…" Yae's face went as red as her underwear as she said that. She buried her face in her hands and crouched down.

The mohawk vanished, and was replaced by her usual hairstyle. It seemed answering really did get rid of our wigs.

*So her underwear is red, huh? If I recall correctly, Yae's a fan of loincloths. Which would mean right now she's wearing a red loincloth.*

My musings were interrupted by Leen, who held out something to me with a grin. I believe she was next in line to answer.

"What're these?"

"Earplugs. I can't sleep at night without them. Good thing I always keep them on me. I don't suppose you could put those in for me, Darling?"

"Nice going, Leen!"

"Why did you not bring those out earlier, why did you not?!" Yae accosted Leen, tears in her eyes. *Tch, I can't believe she had countermeasures in place…* I reluctantly put in the earplugs. Wow, these really block out sound well. I never would have expected a fantasy world's earplugs to be so well designed.

I watched as everyone said the color of their underwear, and their hairstyles returned to normal. *Tsk…*

Hilde was the last to go, and after she'd finished, the die fell to the ground once more.

"It is my turn now, I believe. Hah!" Yae added a hefty spin to the die as she threw it. Almost as if she were venting her frustrations onto the die.

This time the dicen came up on five. *Thank goodness, it looks like we're getting through this pretty fast.*

We went through a whole slew of events, including eating very spicy food without water, dancing for a minute straight, and so on. Each of them were the kinds of things you'd get in a punishment game. Finally, we were only a few spaces from the goal. With plenty of time to spare, too. *We'll be able to make it, right?* Though I was wondering what was taking Paula so long. She should have been able to get Parshe by now.

"Hah!" Leen threw the dicen, and it landed on four.

The marker moved four spaces forward, and like always our surroundings began to morph.

"Whoa?!"

"It's the beach?!" A picturesque view spread out before us. Bright white sand, a clear blue sky, and dazzling sapphire waves as far as the eye could see.

"Is this really all an illusion?"

"The sea breeze smells so real…" Sue ran up to the water's edge and began splashing about in the shallows.

"This must be real. The water feels completely real."

"Hmm…It even tastes salty. I wonder if space-time magic and barrier magic…and summoning magic would be enough to make a fake sea like this." Leen squatted down, dipped her finger into the water, and licked it.

There were wave pools and the like back on Earth, so I guess it shouldn't have been too surprising that magic could replicate an ocean here too. Even I could make waves with water magic.

"This is astounding… Ancient technology really is impressive." Leen was right, this was still quite impressive. Except all this technology was being used to make a board game…

Oh yeah, what were the instructions for this tile again? I looked at the map and read the instructions aloud.

"Change into the designated clothes? Does that mean…"

"I believe it's these… Touya."

"Huh? Oh…" I turned around to see Lu standing next to a clothes rack that had been left lying on the beach. She took one of the outfits and showed it to me.

It was a swimsuit. That's about as cliched as it gets. There was another clothes rack with men's swimsuits. There was even a changing tent.

"Wait! This swimsuit's just a few pieces of string!"

"Apparently it adjusts itself to fit whoever's wearing it. Is this, too, a product of ancient technology?"

"These are all awfully revealing…" The girls gathered around the clothes rack and started looking for swimsuits they liked.

I figured I wouldn't have to be as picky, since I don't much care what I'm wearing. But when I started looking through the rack, I realized most of these were rather bizarre.

*I'm not even sure how to wear this one… It goes in a V-shape down to my crotch…The doctor sure had some strange tastes. And this is just… a single leaf. Just because a comedy group wore it doesn't mean I will!* There was another one that was completely transparent, and another that resembled a very tight speedo. Finally, I managed to find a normal pair of swim trunks.

I headed toward the changing tent, then stopped. It might be a good idea to see what happens when I get these trunks wet first.

After all, knowing the doctor, they might have ended up dissolving in water.

It turned out they were safe, so I went to go change. Inside the tent there was a tiny chest and a small placard next to it that said "Please put your clothes in here once you've changed." Apparently, after a set amount of time, the clothes I was wearing and the clothes in this chest would be swapped. Which meant if I didn't want to end up naked, I better do as the sign said. I put the clothes in the chest and shut the lid. There was an audible click as the chest locked itself. *I am going to get my clothes back later, aren't I?* As I expected, the girls took longer to change. They do realize that if we take too long our time limit'll be up and we'll get thrown out naked right?

"Sorry we took so long, Touya."

"Ah…" Yumina left the tent first. She was wearing a white one-piece suit with a floral design.

Sue came out afterward, clad in a yellow polka-dot one-piece with frills.

Next came Elze and Linze, both wearing standard bikinis. Elze's was red and Linze's was blue.

Next came Yae, wearing a purple ensemble with a pareo wrapped around her. As expected, Yae's bust revealed its true powers when freed from the surly bonds of her sarashi.

Hilde finally came out, though she seemed more than shy. Come to think of it, this was the first time I'd seen Hilde in a swimsuit. She wore a frilly orange bikini. The bottom had a skirt-like design. Hilde wasn't quite on Yae's level, but she had some mighty fine assets.

I wondered why they had their swords, though… Then again, I wasn't one to talk, I'd brought Brunhild with me just in case.

I also looked over to see Lu's swimsuit for the first time. It was an emerald one-piece with a halterneck.

Finally Leen showed up, clad in a frilly black bikini halterneck. She had a more mature atmosphere about her, but it was offset a bit by her childish body. Much like Hilde, the bottom piece of her suit was skirt-like.

"Sorry it took us so long, there was a lot to choose from in there."

"Th-There was one outfit that was just three seashells. What was that doctor thinking…?" *She was thinking something messed up, Elze.*

*Hm?* I smelled something. *What's this?* "What's that nice smell?"

"Oh, it seems like our swimsuits are lightly scented… Not too much, though." It smelled vaguely like citrus, with a bit of mint mixed in. I wondered if this was a normal fragrance in the ancient kingdom. Or maybe it was just something that the swimsuits were designed to have… Though I couldn't help but notice mine didn't have any such scent.

Still, it was a rare opportunity to bring everyone together at the beach. I was a little bit thankful to the pervy old doctor. Though I'd never say something like that out loud.

We all decided to start rolling the dicen again. Just because we'd gotten changed didn't mean the game was over, after all.

"The goal isn't that far off."

"We've still got around thirty minutes. But I'm a little worried about that one space just before the goal…"

"Yeah, it says 'Must Stop'… I wonder what that's all about…" Yumina tilted her head, but clearly had no idea. In typical board games like this, there was often a space near the end that would make you go back to the start.

But this space said 'Must Stop,' not 'Back to the Start'… So I didn't think it was that. *If it actually does restart the game I'm gonna flip the board. I can't afford to miss the goal here.*

Even so, the wicked doctor had made this game. There was no telling what she'd do to screw us over.

"By the way, Touya… It's your turn to roll."

"Hm? Ah, right then. Let's do it."

I took the dice from Lu and threw it on the sandy beach while giving it a vertical spin. It rolled a few times before landing on a six.

*Hell yeah!*

"Wow! We are so close to the goal now, we are!"

Yae jumped around in excitement, making her two *assets* move in a captivating manner. It took an iron will to keep me from staring at them. I noticed that Lu and Yumina were looking at me with reproachful eyes, which made me feel completely cornered.

Anyway, I brought the piece to the "Must Stop" square just before the goal, but the surroundings remained unchanged. *What the hell?*

"Ah! It's saying something?!" Hilde pointed at a large square on the map.

"'Defeat the incoming enemy with only elemental magic?' What enemy?"

As I became puzzled, something appeared from the sea.

At first, it looked like a bluish slime, but a moment later, it actually stood up.

Indeed. It had legs to stand on. Though, I wasn't sure if legs was appropriate, considering they were neither human nor draconic. In fact, they were tentacles, which made the creature look highly… jellyfish-like.

Despite that, I couldn't help but feel that I was looking at a slime from a certain game. Specifically, the one that could use healing magic. I mean… it even had eye-like parts.

It was also pretty damn huge. About as large as Sango in Heavenly Beast mode, in fact. This large slime-jellyfish was twisting its tentacles as it crawled straight towards us.

"Th-That's a King Poison Jelly… Oh no…"

"Leen? You know about this thing?!" Her voice was shaky, so everyone looked at her with worry.

"It's a magic beast with great vitality and tentacles that have both a weak paralyzing poison and a lightning that it uses for offense. King Poison Slimes don't actually attack people, but they're amphibious, and they often go ashore to eat citrus fruits — a favorite of theirs."

"Citrus…? Hold on a second! You don't mean that…" Elze turned pallid and glared at Leen.

"That's exactly what I mean. It's coming towards us because of how we smell right now. Our swimsuits are drenched in the scent of citrus." Leen forced a grin as the rest of us became dumbfounded.

*She played us like a damn fiddle!*

All of us present shared that exact same thought.

That damn pervert had accounted for everything.

"It's coming!" Hilde's cry made everyone split up. She readied her sword, Yae unsheathed her katana, Lu took her twin blades out of her ring's [**Storage**], and Elze equipped her gauntlets from the ring on her neck's chain.

*Wait… Will the magic on them even work?*

"What shall we do?"

"Well, we could distract it by throwing our swimsuits away…"

"There's no way we're doing that!"

"I-I know! I'm just thinking out loud!" Elze turned beet red and strongly rejected my suggestion. Well, it wasn't like I expected her to agree. Still, our actual clothes were in a locked treasure chest.

"Guess we'll have to do it."

"A-Are you sure?" Linze looked at me with an unpleasant expression.

*Hey, I'm with you here. I don't want to fight this crawly, slimy thing, either.*

"You know we're losing if we take too long, right?"

"Uwah… I-I don't want that. **Entwine thus, Ice! Frozen Curse: [Icebind]!**"

"BLRLRLRLRLRLRLR!" The poison jelly raised a weird voice as it detached its freezing tentacles from the rest of its body and escaped Linze's spell.

A moment later, the torn tentacles were exactly as they were before. *Is this regeneration? Or healing magic? The damn thing seems more and more like the slime from the game.*

"BLRRR!" The poison jelly then formed a cross with its tentacles and launched a lightning bolt.

*Whoa! That was close!* "Haah!"

"Yahh!" Hilde's sword and Yae's katana sliced off its tentacles… only for them to regrow again.

"Nhh?!" Yae went in for another cut, but this time, the tentacles remained attached.

*It doesn't work? But that's a blade imbued with blaze?* Upon further inspection, I noticed that Yae's katana was covered in something slimy — likely one of the poison jelly's secretions. Hilde's sword was in a similar state, and it was clear that it had made their blades dull.

Not missing the opening in her defenses, the poison jelly wrapped its tentacle around Yae's leg.

"Wha-?! EHHHHHH?!"

"Yae!" Suddenly, the jelly flipped her around and began swinging, which, of course, made her *things* swing along with her.

*Crap! Get a hold of yourself, Touya!*

Despite being held upside down, Yae didn't let go of her katana, which was a testament to how much of a samurai she was.

Anyway, the poison jelly, likely aiming for her swimsuit, extended another one of its tentacles.

"GYAAAHHH! S-STAY AWAY! STAY AWAY FROM MEEE!" Though her blade couldn't cut, it could still repel, so she used her godlike sword arts to keep the slimy appendages away.

The fact she was doing it despite being upside down seriously impressed me.

"Yae!"

Hilde ran to the tentacles to save Yae.

*Oh, right, I have to help, too!* I fixed Brunhild's sights on the eye-like thing and fired a few bullets at it. I thought that was a weak spot and expected it to suffer great damage, but the bullets merely sank a bit inside and were soon ejected into the sea.

I'd expected the eye-like thing to be a core or something, but when I shot it again, the result was exactly the same. Realizing I was wasting bullets, I decided to shoot the tentacles holding Yae instead, but all I got was a clicking sound.

*I'm out of bullets!*

"[Reload]…! Wait, ah! My bullet pouch is in the chest with my clothes!"

*Damn it! I was too careless! I wasted all my bullets!* Both Linze and Yumina didn't even have their guns, so they obviously didn't have any bullets, either.

"HYAAAHHH!" The scream made me turn, and I saw Hilde, held in the same way as Yae. Hers were the second largest after Yae's, but their swaying was just as tantalizing.

*Crap! Keep a level head, damn it!*

**"Come forth, O Light! Shining Duet: [Light Arrow]!!"** Several bolts of light escaped Linze's hands. A few of them landed on the jelly's head-like part, but it didn't look like they had much of an effect.

"Poison jellies are highly resistant to magic. I don't think even a **[Fire Storm]** could beat it." As we clenched our teeth in frustration, Leen explained why the thing seemed so strong. *Man, no jellyfish should be this much trouble.*

"HYAAAHHH! Hey, you little…! Let me go!"

"KYAAAHHHHHH!" I turned to the screams again and noticed that both Elze and Lu had joined Yae and Hilde in hanging. After looking at and comparing the sizes of their swaying chests, I concluded that the new entries weren't particularly distracting.

"Dunno why, but I'm kinda angry!"

"Same here." *Oh no, they noticed the intricacies of my gaze and began directing some sort of dark aura towards me.*

Thankfully, they were too preoccupied with deflecting the tentacles reaching for their swimsuits, so the aura soon began to disperse.

*Phew.*

Still, the situation was dire. If I charged in with Brunhild, I'd end up just like Yae.

*I could do something if Null magic was allowed, but…* "Touya, something has me curious…"

"What is it, Sue?" I turned to her, hoping to hear some sort of weak point she'd figured out.

"I'm merely wondering why you don't call Kohaku and the others. Can't we use summoning magic here?" **"…Come forth, Darkness. Bring out my Desired Heavenly Beasts of Covenant: [Sango, Kokuyo]…!"**

*Hey, I didn't forget, okay?* I formed a magic circle on the beach, and it soon began releasing a black mist. A few moments later, the mist cleared, leaving Sango and Kokuyo floating in its place. Considering our enemy, I felt that these two were a better choice than Kohaku and the rest.

"It's rare of you to sssummon usss, masster."

"Hm? Are we inside a subspace?"

"Sango, Kokuyo, can you do anything about that thing?" The spirit turtle and black snake *slowly* turned to where I was pointing and then, with a pop of smoke, returned to their true forms.

*Is it just me, or are they bigger than before?* "Massster, mind telling usss what we are looking at?"

"Wah?!"

"Hyah?!"

"Bhuh?!"

"Kyah?!" After a single glare from Kokuyo, the poison jelly let go of the girls, creating four splashes.

It also felt like the jellyfish started shaking and became pale.

*Or was it always like that?*

Sango took another step forward.

"I don't know the circumstances, but you seem to have mistreated our master's ladies."

"Ohh dear me, that'sss not ssomething we can tolerate, isss it? You ready for what'sss about to happen?" Kokuyo's dagger-sharp words made the poison jelly squirm and run to the sea at incredible speeds. *I think it's actually running on water.*

"DON'T YOU DARE RUN FROM ME, YOU LITTLE SHIT!!!" Following the shout, Kokuyo launched a blade of water that quickly reached the poison jelly and split it in half.

*It's pretty impressive that its power didn't drop from this range.*

As I stared in amazement, Sango and Kokuyo returned to their mini forms.

"Master, ladies. We took care of the lout, so rest easy."

"Hey now, Sssango dearesst, I'm the one who took care of it. Massster, any praisse you're giving sshould go to me."

"Thanks, you two." I expressed my gratitude and pet their heads. Suddenly, both of them disappeared. Thinking that they were forcefully unsummoned, I tried calling them again, but the magic seemed to be sealed again.

*Oh crap, I almost forgot about the girls.* They dropped in the water after a while of hanging upside down, so I had to check on them.

"Wait, stop right there! Touya! Don't move from where you are!"

"Eh?" Hilde popped her head out of the sea and told me to stay away. *What?* "M-My swimsuit was taken by the water when I fell! Please stay there until I find it!!!"

"S-Same here…"

*What?!* The girls on the beach went to help Hilde and Yae search for their swimsuits.

Elze and Lu were just fine, though… *Did it have something to do with size? Impacts cause wilder shaking when they're big, so maybe that made it slip to the side and…* I looked away from the sea and considered the important things.

After some time, the swimsuits and the clothes in the treasure chest should be exchanged, but we were on a limit here. That damn jellyfish sure was a time waster.

Speaking of that thing, it was the enemy sent after us, so defeating it gave us the dice.

"Well, the next square is the goal, so we're rising up regardless of what we get."

"Sorry for the wait!" I turned to the voices coming from the sea and saw Hilde in her complete swimsuit again. Yae, however, was hiding her chest with a purple cloth tied around it. *Is that her pareo? So they didn't find it, huh?*

"Let's hurry, Touya. They've been poisoned by the jelly."

"What?!"

"It's paralysis poison. Really weak, too, so its effects should go away with time, but we should still reach the goal as soon as possible." Leen explained the situation while looking at the affected girls, who were all sitting down. According to Yae, it felt like the leg the jelly grabbed had gone numb, and she compared it to a long time sitting in an uncomfortable position, and it didn't sound the least bit pleasant.

I took the dice, rolled it, and got a one, putting us right on the goal. We had a total of three minutes left, so it was safe to say that we made it.

The piece moved to the goal, which caused the scenery to change. We all felt the switch overwhelm our senses, but the result was perplexing, as it was just another beach.

"Eh?!" I couldn't help but voice my shock. After all, there was a gate saying "GOAL" about a hundred meters away from the shoreline.

*Eh?! Just reaching the goal square wasn't enough?!*

"H-Hey, can you girls run?!"

"Th-That would be a harsh task…" Yae answered with a forced smile. *What do I do? Sue, Leen, and Yumina wouldn't be able to carry the paralyzed girls, meaning that I was the only one who could do it!*

"Linze! Take Yumina and the rest and carry Lu to the goal!"

"O-Okay!" Lu was the most petite of the four, so she wouldn't have been that much of a problem for them.

"I'll carry the rest! You first, Elze!"

"Eh! Wh-? Me?! Hyah?!" Ignoring her protests, I took her from the side and raised her up in the so-called "princess carry."

Not a second later, I started running towards the goal.

*Khh… Sand isn't easy to run on, and she's actually heavier than I tho—* I felt a sudden pressure on my skin. Elze's silent stare hurt me deeply. The feeling of her skin on mine made my heart beat, but I tried my best to ignore it and just run.

Upon reaching the goal, I placed Elze on the sand and dashed back to the other girls.

On my way, I passed by Lu, being carried by the four unparalyzed girls. They did it by holding a limb each, and it didn't look the least bit pleasant, but there was nothing that could be done about this.

I raised Hilde from her sitting position and carried her on my back. Dashing a hundred meters while princess carrying was really taxing, so I decided to switch to this.

"T-Touya… A-Am I not heavy…?"

"Nooo, not at all. This is nothing… to me…" Despite what I said, my breath was becoming ragged.

*Man, I've been relying on* [**Boost**] *too much recently. I should really work out more…*

The poor surface, the blazing sun, and the two mounds pushing against my back tired me both physically and mentally. Her breasts weren't touching me directly, but there was only a single piece of cloth separating us, meaning that it wasn't hard for me to feel both their softness and warmth.

Somehow hiding the pounding in my chest, I successfully brought Hilde to the goal.

That left only Yae. Right as the girls finished carrying Lu, I dashed back to Yae, and it was becoming really hard on my lungs and stamina.

I picked up Yae the same way I did Hilde. Her large — clearly bigger than Hilde's — breasts attacked my back, but the pareo over them was thick enough to make them significantly less powerful than Hilde's. *I can bear this.*

"A-Are you all right, Touya-dono?!"

"I… I'm… Fine!" I could barely even talk at this point. Honestly, I was probably at my limit. My legs were shaking, and I felt like I could trip at any moment, but I went too far to fall now, so I mustered my vigor and continued moving forward.

*I'm so close…!* My leg sank into the sand, making me tilt forward. The goal was just a few steps away, so I decided to jump towards it.

"Hyah?!"

"Bgrh!" Yae's weight overwhelmed me. As my face became buried in the sand, someone took me by the arm and pulled me in.

*Ow ow ow, hot hot hot!* Apparently, my leg was still outside the goal. They could've been a bit more gentle, though…

"W-We made it…"

"That was close." Linze's and Sue's voices made me look up and see that the countdown was stuck at one second. *That was too close for comfort…*

"Congratulations on reaching the goal. Unfortunately, you are victorious. I will now send you back to where you were. Feel free to play again whenever you have the chance." Dr. Babylon's voice resounded from out of nowhere, and the hot sand beneath my face was replaced with a cold floor. We cleared the game and came back to the Storehouse.

The swimsuits we were wearing were replaced by our original clothing.

"**[R-Refresh]**…" I cast a stamina-healing spell on myself. Energy re-filled my body, and the lethargy from before vanished like it was never there.

"Oh man…" That was horrible. That pervy doctor had no intention of letting us reach the goal.

"I'm sooo tired… Touya, refresh me too…"

"M-Myself, as well, please."

"Same…" All the girls were tired, so I didn't hesitate in complying.

After that, I took a look at the dice on the floor.

"Yeah, we're sealing this away. This artifact is a menace." I put it in the Storehouse's safe box and locked it inside. As I breathed a tired sigh, I suddenly heard hysteric voices from behind me.

"Eh?"

"Wha—?!"

"Heah?!" I turned around and saw the girls touch their own bodies, as if looking for something that's missing.

*Wh-What?*

"Wh-Why? Why?!"

"Hey, what's wrong…?"

"STOOOP! Touya, don't move from where you are! Stay, boy!"

*What am I, a dog?*

Still, I did as she told and stood still. *What happened?*

"…Let me ask you one thing, darling. When we changed to our swimsuits, did you put your clothes in the treasure chest?"

"Eh? Well, I did, yeah." I answered Leen's question as honestly as I could.

*If I didn't place my clothes there, I wouldn't have gotten them back, right?*

"And did you put your underwear in the underwear box?"

"What? I don't remember anything like that."

"Khhh… There's the problem. We've been tricked." Leen, her cheeks rosy, clicked her tongue. *What does she mean?* "Our tent had a chest for clothes *and* a chest for underwear… And we were wondering why there were two, but…"

"Eh?"

"We didn't get our underwear back." Sue told it like it was, and the rest of the girls turned red and hung their heads.

*Eh? So they're all going commando right n—?*

"T-Touya, you turn around and count to a hundred! Look at us and I'm punching you!"

"Ah, s-sure!" I quickly turned and heard them all run out of the room. *That damn pervy doctor never does anything good, does she? Wait, am I really supposed to count to hundred all by myself? This is making me feel empty.*

*But wait, what happened to their underwear? Could it be that...?*

I looked towards the sealed dice.

*...Touya, no. Discard your wicked thoughts. They lead only to ruin.*

I began counting unnecessarily loudly.

Once done with that, I got curious about Paula and went to the alchemy tower, where I saw her vigorously gesturing to Flora and Parshe.

"Table? Book? Hmm... I don't really get it."

"I think-a she's talking about windows. Square windows!" She was probably trying to tell them about the dice, but the two were too dense to figure it out.

Hell, she didn't even have to tell them anything. She could've just pulled them over...

I tapped her shoulder to tell her that it's enough, but for some reason, that just made her irritated and got her to gesture with even more intensity.

Later, I'd heard that Paula was seen doing a heated one-man show, which, in my opinion, showed just how much of a hard-worker she was.

*This afterword was written before the broadcast of the In Another World With My Smartphone anime adaptation.*

Finally, we're up to volume eight of In Another World With My Smartphone. It's me again, Patora Fuyuhara. Did you enjoy the volume? I thought this one was quite fun, so I hope you feel the same.

I guess I wanna talk about something first. It's already been revealed, but… We're getting an anime! I'm glad I can finally say it… I've been holding in that knowledge for a while, you know. It still doesn't feel real, if I'm being honest.

I was writing on my smartphone as usual, then I took a nap around noon.

Suddenly my phone started buzzing out of the blue. I looked at my phone and noticed it was already three in the afternoon, so I quickly picked it up. The caller was K, from HJ Books.

About a week before that, we'd gone over details for the manga adaptation of Smartphone, we'd also had many calls and e-mails about details to do with the setting such as names and so on. I just assumed it was going to be something else like that, so I picked up.

"Mh… Hello…?"

"Ah, hey there. This is K from HJ. Sorry for disturbing you, is it alright if we talk now?"

"I was just taking a little nap, that's all… I can talk alright, so don't worry."

"Hahaha... Actually, we were thinking of adapting Smartphone into an anime. I was calling to see if I could get your permission for that, Mr. Fuyuhara."

"............ Huh? Whuh?"

"An anime. Are you alright?"

"...Oh, I'm still asleep, huh... What a weird dream."

"That's not it!" He was laughing, but I was having trouble wrapping my own head around what was being said. An anime? Not just a manga? What was happening here?

"The details aren't sorted out fully yet, but we won't be going ahead without your permission." He was moving along way too fast for me. I hadn't even come to terms with what he'd said, but he was asking for my consent. I wanted him to slow down!

I wasn't used to dealing with stuff like this... I'd only just given the go-ahead for the manga, after all, and that wasn't even announced yet. My head was spinning. My chest was fit to burst.

"Well, at any rate. I'd like you to come over to the office next week, is that alright?"

"Huh? In Tokyo?"

"Yep. We can have a proper meeting about the anime adaptation." He was dead serious... He was totally serious!

And so, the week after, I headed into Tokyo. I had a meeting with Hobby Japan's editorial department about getting an anime adaptation for Smartphone.

I talked to various people about various things. HJ's staff wanted to cover things like staff, studio, contract details, and so on... In the end I just let the relevant people deal with the relevant details.

But now you all know the truth! An anime for Smartphone... It's incredible. They just decided on it, just like that. It seemed like the decision to adapt Smartphone into an anime, and the decision to adapt Smartphone into a manga, had both progressed separately. They just coincidentally happened to settle around the same time. So one week it was "We're doing a manga!", and then the next week it was "We're doing an anime!"

It was like that old proverb about water in your ear. It's shocking when you notice it, but sometimes it had been there for a while.

Since then I've been keeping up with a lot of e-mails about the anime, the manga, and of course the novel series as well.

Plus I've been continuing to write In Another World With My Smartphone in its web novel format while making edits to my old material before it gets novelized properly.

Since I heard about the anime, I've been writing a little more excitedly. I've been picturing the world moving inside my mind. Minor characters who didn't have much of an established appearance will get character designs, too! Even that makes me happy.

Honestly part of me still thinks this could be an elaborate or cruel prank, but I doubt they'd go to such lengths...

Anyway, the details about the anime will be released at a later date on Hobby Japan's website. I can't wait! I really hope you all enjoy it... Who knows, if it's successful we could get lots of new things.

Now, it's time for my special thanks.

Eiji Usatsuka, thanks for your illustrations as always. I'm so grateful to you for bringing my writing to life. I think your character designs are going to look amazing when they're animated.

Tomofumi Ogasawara, your Frame Gear designs become more incredible every time I see a new one. I look forward to working with you in Volume Nine as well.

To K, my most humble of thanks for being the brilliant bridge between my work and not just a manga adaptation, but now an anime adaptation. I'm astounded every day at how lucky I am.

As usual, thank you to everyone involved in the publication of this book. Thank you so much to the editorial staff.

To everyone involved with the anime adaptation of my work, I'm indebted to you in so many ways.

And all of those who supported me on "Shousetsuka ni Narou," as well as the dear readers of this book, you have my deepest gratitude.

Well, for now... Let's meet again in Volume Nine of In Another World With My Smartphone.

Patora Fuyuhara

# The White Knight
## 《Shining Count》

Developer: Regina Babylon (Modified by Rosetta)     Chief Engineer: Rosetta
Maintainer: Monica                                  Affiliation: Brunhild
Compatible Pilots: Lain

Height: 16.6m     Weight: 7.7t     Maximum Capacity: 1 Person

Armaments: Standard Sword, Shield, Mace, Battlehammer, Lance, Halberd, Battle Axe.
One of the Anti-Phrase Weapons, a Frame Gear. A modded version of the Knight Baron.
It was developed for Lain upon her promotion to commander of Brunhild's knight order.
It is effectively the flagship unit of Brunhild's army.
While it looks different to the standard black knight unit, it is functionally identical in performance.

Another World With My Smartphone

ra Fuyuhara
ation・Eiji Usatsuka

9

ON SALE
APRIL 2020!

# J-Novel Club Lineup

## Ebook Releases Series List

Amagi Brilliant Park
An Archdemon's Dilemma:
   How to Love Your Elf Bride
Arifureta Zero
Arifureta: From Commonplace
   to World's Strongest
Ascendance of a Bookworm
Bluesteel Blasphemer
Campfire Cooking in Another World
   with My Absurd Skill
Cooking with Wild Game
Crest of the Stars
Demon King Daimaou
Demon Lord, Retry!
Der Werwolf: The Annals of Veight
From Truant to Anime Screenwriter: My
   Path to "Anohana" and "The Anthem of
   the Heart"
Full Metal Panic!
Grimgar of Fantasy and Ash
How a Realist Hero Rebuilt the Kingdom
How NOT to Summon a Demon Lord
I Saved Too Many Girls and Caused the
   Apocalypse
I Shall Survive Using Potions!
If It's for My Daughter, I'd Even Defeat a
   Demon Lord
In Another World With My Smartphone
Infinite Dendrogram
Infinite Stratos
Invaders of the Rokujouma!?
JK Haru is a Sex Worker in Another World
Kokoro Connect
Last and First Idol
Lazy Dungeon Master
Middle-Aged Businessman, Arise in Another
   World!
Mixed Bathing in Another Dimension
My Big Sister Lives in a Fantasy World
My Next Life as a Villainess: All Routes Lead
   to Doom!
Otherside Picnic
Outbreak Company
Paying to Win in a VRMMO

Record of Wortenia War
Seirei Gensouki: Spirit Chronicles
Seriously Seeking Sister! Ultimate Vampire
   Princess Just Wants Little Sister; Plenty of
   Service Will Be Provided!
Sexiled: My Sexist Party Leader Kicked
   Me Out, So I Teamed Up With a Mythical
   Sorceress!
Side-By-Side Dreamers
Sorcerous Stabber Orphen:
   The Wayward Journey
The Faraway Paladin
The Greatest Magicmaster's Retirement Plan
The Magic in this Other World is
   Too Far Behind!
The Master of Ragnarok & Blesser of Einherjar
The Unwanted Undead Adventurer
There Was No Secret Evil-Fighting
   Organization (srsly?!), So I Made One
   MYSELF!
Welcome to Japan, Ms. Elf!

### Manga Series:

A Very Fairy Apartment
An Archdemon's Dilemma:
   How to Love Your Elf Bride
Animeta!
Ascendance of a Bookworm
Cooking with Wild Game
Demon Lord, Retry!
Discommunication
How a Realist Hero Rebuilt the Kingdom
I Shall Survive Using Potions!
Infinite Dendrogram
Marginal Operation
Seirei Gensouki: Spirit Chronicles
Sorcerous Stabber Orphen:
   The Reckless Journey
Sweet Reincarnation
The Faraway Paladin
The Magic in this Other World is
   Too Far Behind!
The Master of Ragnarok & Blesser of Einherjar
The Unwanted Undead Adventurer